THE WESLEYAN THEOLOGY SERIES

Creation

Eric M. Vail

THE FOUNDRY
PUBLISHING

Copyright © 2022 by Eric M. Vail
The Foundry Publishing®
PO Box 419527
Kansas City, MO 64141
thefoundrypublishing.com

978-0-8341-4119-3

All rights reserved. No part of this publication may be reproduced, stored in a retrieval system, or transmitted in any form or by any means—for example, electronic, photocopy, recording—without the prior written permission of the publisher. The only exception is brief quotations in printed reviews.

Cover design: Arthur Cherry
Interior design: Sharon Page

Library of Congress Cataloging-in-Publication Data
A complete catalog record for this book is available from the Library of Congress.

All Scripture quotations, unless indicated, are taken from THE HOLY BIBLE, NEW INTERNATIONAL VERSION®, NIV® Copyright © 1973, 1978, 1984, 2011 by Biblica, Inc.® Used by permission. All rights reserved worldwide.

The following copyrighted versions are used by permission:

The New American Standard Bible® (NASB), Copyright © 1960, 1971, 1977, 1995, 2020 by The Lockman Foundation. All rights reserved.

The New Revised Standard Version Bible (NRSV), copyright © 1989 the Division of Christian Education of the National Council of the Churches of Christ in the United States of America. Used by permission. All rights reserved.

The *Contemporary English Version* (CEV). Copyright © by American Bible society 1991, 1992. Used by permission.

The *Holy Bible*, New Living Translation (NLT), copyright © 1996, 2004, 2015. Used by permission of Tyndale House Publishers, Inc., Wheaton, Illinois 60189. All rights reserved.

The internet addresses, email addresses, and phone numbers in this book are accurate at the time of publication. They are provided as a resource. The Foundry Publishing does not endorse them or vouch for their content or permanence.

*To D. Lyle Dabney, whose impact on my
theological perspective continues to this day*

Contents

Acknowledgments   7
1. Driving Reflections   9
2. Ancient Outlooks   21
3. Genesis 1: Beginning   35
4. Genesis 1: Dwelling   67
5. Old Testament Voices   99
6. Creation in the New Testament   121
7. An Unfolding Tradition   143
8. Creation Imagination   173

Acknowledgments

How could I have known the first week I started teaching at MVNU and Alex Varughese asked me to write *Atonement and Salvation* that this *Wesleyan Theology Series* was going to define the first decade of my teaching career? As I have moved from that first book, to *Eschatology*, and now *Creation*, it has been a delight to immerse myself in the narrative arc of God with us and God for us. It feels less like I have been a contributor to this series than this series has contributed to me and to the work I do as a teacher and pastor. Thank you, Alex Varughese and Bonnie Perry, for entrusting me with these volumes.

This is the third volume for which I have been able to dialogue with Alex Varughese and Al Truesdale through the writing process. I am thankful to them for pushing me. Not only do they help strengthen the final product, but I also come to new insights through the exchange. Thanks also to Ben Boeckel for sharing his knowledge on the literary structure of Genesis. This has been my second opportunity to work with Audra Spiven on the final edits, and I thank her for her contributions.

I am thankful that MVNU granted me a sabbatical in the spring of 2019, during which I was able to complete a great deal of the reading and half of the writing for this volume. They were gracious in letting me pivot to this project on the eve of my sabbatical when it came my way.

Lastly, I am thankful for the wonderful support of my family, who give me the space to do this work. My colleagues and students are a great encouragement to me as well. I am grateful to be surrounded by such a supportive community.

ONE

Driving Reflections

My own love for camping and hiking—especially in national parks—was cemented when I lived in Kings Canyon National Park in California for two summers during my college years. Having the Sierra Nevada as my playground made my hours at a humble summer job worth it. I logged hundreds of miles hiked and thousands of feet climbed in my attempt to take in the features of the park: starry nights, mountain vistas, alpine lakes, surging rivers, giant sequoias, flowering meadows, and the many animal species. The beauty and vastness of God's creation never failed to delight me in every journey I took. I wanted to see *everything*. I still do! No matter our personal approach to the outdoors, it is likely that, at some time or another, each of us has been awed by its wonders and moved to offer words of praise and thanksgiving to its Creator.

Different experiences can spark our thoughts about God as our Creator. With all the tools we have for looking into outer space, we may lose our breath not only because of the beauty but also due to how vast all the distances are, the sheer size and number of objects, and the mind-blowing forces at work in the universe. These considerations may lead us to reflect about the God who could create on such a massive scale. Perhaps we may equally marvel at the smallest details we can observe. Whether we are investigating subatomic particles or the smallest structures of our world, there is astounding complexity in the tiniest of features. It is humbling to think of our Creator taking such thoughtful care of the little details. Beyond the big and small, any number of pleasures from all our senses and experiences of life could lead us to delight in God's masterful artistry and generosity. It is easy to be thankful to God for the beauty and many joys of creation. God's reliability may comfort us as we live year by year through the cycle of seasons or as we note the regularity of physical properties in the world. And ever-new delights, never exactly like before, may lead us to celebrate the unfolding journey of God with the world. So many things may lead us toward thinking about the character of our Creator and toward worship.

It is a privilege to have these times of reflection and worship—these moments that halt our labor. It is especially a privilege if we have extended time to reflect. Yet few people around the world have the luxury of time and stockpiled resources that would allow them to sit and contemplate anything that does not have to do with meeting basic needs or pressing concerns. As we address the demands of our days, it is possible to be struck with amazement at a glimpse of a sunset, the smell of rain, a singing bird, the taste of honey, or the tickle of snowflakes on our faces. Yet, most often, the more urgent issues of life get our attention. Moments to reflect, to indulge our curiosity, or to delight in God are not necessarily what dominate our days. Sweet moments are a blessing beyond our daily needs.

There are, however, life experiences that may make our reflections about our Creator more urgent and all-consuming. Crisis moments leave little room for savoring and delighting. It is difficult, in a crisis, to think beyond the intensity of the moment. Our thoughts and prayers during crises are less a pastime or luxury than critical cries for deliverance. These cries hold in them the weight of our lives and futures. So much more is at stake about who God is when we are being crushed. It is not a matter of curiosity who God is; it is a matter of salvation. While we may at first think the doctrine of creation belongs to moments of peaceful reflection—as a surplus doctrine for a surplus time—its real home is in the high-stakes times of crisis. Instead of speculative thoughts about God, God's identity matters most at those critical points, when who God *really is* matters *right now*.

In the history of Israel, they did not immediately start writing down beliefs about God as Creator. Rather, at first they were journeying with God and getting to know God across a history of profound events. God called Abraham and Sarah, made promises to them in a binding covenant, and gave them a child who was otherwise impossible for them to have. As their descendants became more numerous and were bound to Egypt in slavery, God not only delivered them and cemented their future in a covenant, but God also gave them their inheritance of the land of Canaan. Israel's memories of these historic moments of promise and salvation were the foundation for their present existence and their hoped-for future.[1] God's faithfulness through each stage in their history gave them confidence that God would ultimately fulfill every covenant promise. Thus, through much of Israel's history, the source of their confidence was not a belief about God as Creator—a topic that predated their lived experience with God.[2] Instead, they lived according to what they knew firsthand; they had no reason to doubt their Redeemer, who always had been a faithful Companion.

Eventually, however, a national crisis made Israel question God and whether their confidence in God's character and ability had been warranted. The crisis pressed them to

---

1. Jürgen Moltmann, *Theology of Hope: On the Ground and the Implications of a Christian Eschatology*, trans. James W. Leitch (Minneapolis: Fortress Press, 1993), 297.

2. Moltmann, *Theology of Hope*, 298.

think beyond their experience and question the broader categories about God as the world's Creator and the nature of creation itself. That crisis was Babylon's invasion, which climaxed with the destruction of Jerusalem and Solomon's Temple (in 587/6 BCE). God's covenant people were led away into captivity in Babylon. Their world—and, it seemed, their future—had been stripped away. During their exile, they had many reasons to doubt God's place in the world, the extent of God's power, the dependability of God's promises, and the goodness of God's character. Was their God really Lord of all? Was their God only a small player in the world? Had they witnessed God being defeated by Babylon's chief god? Was God incapable of delivering on God's promises? Did their downfall mean God was unfaithful and God's promises void? Or could God still be King of kings and this devastation be God's act of judgment against them?[3]

During their *present* crisis—when they had every reason to doubt God and the *future* of God's covenant with them—they confirmed their views about Creator and creation. What they said was based on what they had learned of God in their history. They learned to affirm the nature of God as Creator and the character of the salvation this Creator would bring precisely when such statements seemed contradictory to their crushing circumstances, just

---

3. See Thomas W. Mann, "Stars, Sprouts, and Streams: The Creative Redeemer of Second Isaiah," *God Who Creates: Essays in Honor of W. Sibley Towner*, ed. William P. Brown and S. Dean McBride, Jr. (Grand Rapids: Eerdmans, 2000), 136. David L. Peterson notes that the prophets were not the first people in Israel's history to say anything about creation. It is not as though they did not have a tradition from which to draw. At the same time, "There has been something of a consensus that creation traditions were only important fairly late in Israelite religion and literature. Though this consensus is breaking up, it remains the case that the most powerful exemplar of creation language in prophetic literature occurs in what has hitherto been known as Deutero- or Second Isaiah, prophetic poetry dating to the mid-sixth century B.C.E." (Peterson, "The World of Creation in the Book of the Twelve," *God Who Creates*, 206f.).

as Christians later affirmed God's power in Christ's cross and Christ's enthronement during their own persecution. In their time of crisis it truly mattered to Israel whether God is the incomparable, uncontestable Creator of all there is—that the Creator surpasses anything in all creation. Who God is as Creator had direct bearing on the salvation they could expect. While it may seem backward, the *future* was in question when they reflected on the beginning.

The Hebrew word *bara* ("create") is celebrated as a key Old Testament word for God's unique capacity to create. The second part of Isaiah (chapters 40–66), which was written during and after Israel's exile, "is likely among the first (if not the first) of all biblical writings to use the verb *bārā'* to speak of God as creator."[4] It was a bold affirmation that rose up within Israel in the midst of their crisis. Modern scholars also date the writing of Genesis 1 to the time period around Israel's exile—after they had experienced both devastation and the promise of redemption.[5] From this perspective, Genesis 1:1–2:3 then refers "to the original act of creation but in terms of the questions of the exilic community concerning the fate of Israel."[6] What would it mean for the God who has created from the beginning to create Israel anew out of complete desolation? Even though it stands at the beginning of the Bible, the probable age of Genesis 1 places it among several capstone statements in

---

4. Mann, "Stars, Sprouts, and Streams," 136. Mann divides Isaiah into First Isaiah (chapters 1–39) and Second Isaiah (chapters 40–66). Some scholars divide Isaiah into three parts, chapters 1–39, 40–54, and 55–66. In the three-part division, the writing of the third portion is attributed to the time when Israel returned to the promised land after exile.

5. Biblical authorship is a popular topic of debate, and it is prudent to acknowledge here that ancient tradition dates Genesis far earlier, attributing the book to Moses. However, modern scholars have mostly moved on from that assumption.

6. Andrew R. Angel, *Chaos and the Son of Man: The Hebrew* Chaoskampf *Tradition in the Period 515 BCE to 200 CE* (London: T & T Clark, 2006), 11. Angel is explaining the view of Richard J. Clifford here.

the Old Testament about the Creator and creation. These various passages represent Israel's faith in God during their exile. Thus, these texts served as assurances about God in Israel's *present* crisis, upon which their hopes for the *future* were justified.

Based on Israel's own experience of crisis that led them to explore what it means to say God is Creator, we can see that the doctrine of creation in the Bible is not *solely* interested in saying how the world came to be.[7] The doctrine was not for the sake of curiosity about the past, nor was it worked out in a relaxed time when God's relationship to the world was not of immediate importance. Even in the early history of Christianity, "the Christian development of this doctrine is less concerned with how the world came to be than with how it is sustained and governed."[8] These Christian writings were for the sake of stating our *present* life with our Creator.

In keeping with the biblical background, the doctrine of creation is first a reflection on God, answering not only, "Who is this God to whom we pray?" but also, "Who is the God who will come to our aid in [our] time of need?"[9] The Scriptures again and again link God as Creator with God as Redeemer. God's power and loving-kindness as our Creator is our *present* hope and assurance in God as our Redeemer.[10] In their history, Israel saw God's loving-kindness at work in significant acts of redemption. That precious history came to be nestled in broader affirmations about God as Creator. Whatever mighty acts God has done as Creator, God can

---

7. Gary A. Anderson, "*Creatio ex nihilo* and the Bible," *Creation* ex nihilo: *Origins, Development, Contemporary Challenges*, ed. Gary A. Anderson and Markus Bockmuehl (Notre Dame, IN: University of Notre Dame Press, 2018), 22.

8. Markus Bockmuehl, "Introduction," *Creation* ex nihilo, 4.

9. Janet Soskice, "Why *Creatio ex nihilo* for Theology Today?" *Creation* ex nihilo, 41.

10. Soskice, "Why *Creatio ex nihilo*?", 41.

do now to create new, life-affirming situations in the world. God's present creative work brings salvation in our circumstances. Moreover, whatever creative acts God is doing now, we know God can and will bring them one day to their ultimate fulfillment.

If there is a dominant biblical theme about God as Creator, it is that God is *Ruler*. All things are under the scope of God's governance; God legislates, administrates, and judges. As this theme ripples across the Scriptures, God is not both queen bee and worker bees all in one. Rather, the world is full of actors, over whom God has authority. God's rule is positive for the world, since God is loving, just, and wise. Creation's Ruler is also majestic and regal. When God appears, creation quakes at God's greatness. As the world's Ruler-Creator, God is unequaled, unsurpassable, and unshakeable. As the Nicene Creed opens: "We believe in one God, the Father, the Almighty, maker of heaven and earth, of all that is, seen and unseen."

Even so, Israel did not affirm that God is simply raw power and might, even more ferocious and destructive than the empires of Egypt, Assyria, or Babylon. God is also not *coldly* just and wise. All of God's power and authority are characterized with affirmations that God is faithful, loving, and nurturing. "The Lord is good to all; he has compassion on all he has made" (Ps. 145:9). Our Ruler is caretaker and savior for creation.

From the Old Testament to the New, God's roles as Ruler, Creator, and Redeemer are inseparably interwoven with one another. The Nicene Creed captures this too. First, each of the three Persons of the Trinity are named in God's creative activity: the Father as "maker of heaven and earth," the Son as the one "through whom all things were made," and the Spirit as "the Lord, the giver of life." These affirmations about the triune God as Creator frame the Creed's middle claims about God's work in Christ—what God is doing "for us and for our salvation." God is not Creator, or Almighty, in order to act for God's self-interest. Rather, the Almighty Creator is the very one acting "for us and for our salvation." As the apostle Paul suggests in Philippians 2:4–11, it is precisely because it is God's nature to work for the benefit of others that the divine Son emptied himself to become human and suffer crucifixion.[11] *The character of divine power is revealed in God's care, even to the point of enduring suffering and death.* While, in the distorted thinking of the world, this may seem weak or foolish, God's loving-care is powerfully effective; it is divinely powerful.

Beyond just our salvation, all God's activities in the Creed have everlasting implications for the coming of God's kingdom and "the life of the world to come." Divine creative dominion functions faithfully, lovingly, and nurturingly for creation's everlasting well-being. God's love is the very life of the world. The Bible teaches further that the nurturing care God has for creation also expresses itself in play, joy, and delight. The relationship between God and creation is not all business. Creator and creation are meant to enjoy each other without end.

Under the umbrella of God as Ruler, there are many metaphors used in the Bible to describe God's creative work. The metaphors run the spectrum of human occupations: artist, craftsperson, farmer, cheesemaker, designer, textile worker, stylist, builder, smith, midwife, teacher, etc. The use of these metaphors means that "create" (*bara*) is not the only creation-related verb that is used in the Bible. God establishes, makes, founds, and forms.[12] God speaks, fills, breathes,

---

11. See Michael J. Gorman, *Cruciformity: Paul's Narrative Spirituality of the Cross* (Grand Rapids: Eerdmans, 2001); and Gorman, *Inhabiting the Cruciform God: Kenosis, Justification, and Theosis in Paul's Narrative Soteriology* (Grand Rapids: Eerdmans, 2009).

12. James L. Mays, "'Maker of Heaven and Earth': Creation in the Psalms," *God Who Creates*, 76.

separates, stretches out, sets boundaries, and blesses. Metaphors abound: God hems in with protection, weaves, knits, fashions, clothes, pours, curdles, and delivers.[13] God's creative provision also waters, quenches, gives drink, makes a way, brings out, and sprouts.[14] If we only did a word study for "create" in the Bible, we would miss the majority of the passages that speak about God's creative activity and relationship to the world as Creator. But importantly, in all the diversity, God is the one who governs the processes of creation. God is creation's Ruler. This affirmation gave confidence to Israel that God could and would come through for God's precious handiwork—whether it was possible for them to see it in their crisis or not. It sure looked to Israel at the time like Babylon had the upper hand.

Facets of the Doctrine

This is a book on the doctrine of creation. The word "creation" can have different meanings in English. It can refer to all that God makes (i.e., the stuff; the heavens and the earth). Alternatively, it can refer to God's action of *making*. This book could focus solely on the origin of everything (God's action). There is a history in Western cultures, going all the way back to the Greek philosophers, of focusing on the question about origins and the existence of everything. This ancient question has two sides: How does the underlying cause of everything *give* being (existence), and how does everything *receive* being from the underlying cause?[15] Through the centuries, many answers have been given about

---

13. William P. Brown, "*Creatio Corporis* and the Rhetoric of Defense in Job 10 and Psalm 139," *God Who Creates*, 110–12, 118.

14. Mann, "Stars, Sprouts, and Streams," 146–49.

15. This question about *being*, and an example of how this question has shaped Christian conversation on the doctrine of creation through the centuries, can be seen in the introduction Steven E. Baldner and William E. Carroll wrote for their translations in *Medieval Sources in Translation 35* (Toronto: Pontifical Institute of Mediaeval Studies, 1997), 4.

the source or cause of our existence. Christians have consistently entered into conversation with Western culture on the question of origins. This discussion has tended to focus our doctrine of creation on that issue of our beginning—specifically, coming into being. Indeed, it is common to summarize the whole doctrine of creation with the belief that God *created out of nothing* (or with the Latin equivalent: *creatio ex nihilo*). However, as we have already seen, reflections about the doctrine of creation are not only about coming into being, the beginning point, or issues about the past. Claims about origins are connected to other ideas.

First, across history, within each suggestion about the origin of existence—when, where, how, and even who—is also a suggestion about the nature of *what* comes to exist (the creation itself). This breadth gives us a history of different views on the structure and dynamics of the heavens and earth, including if there is any *meaning* or *purpose* to the existence of all things. The doctrine of creation cannot help but deal with these additional issues of *what* God creates and *why*. Second, the doctrine is not only about the past, or the first moments in time. It wrestles with questions about our *present*—what we are meant to be and how we are meant to live in the world. Third, the doctrine of creation even deals with creation's *future*. When thinking about *what* creation is and *why* God would create, these are a matter of God's *aim*, the direction in which God has always and ever will be intending for creation to go—that is, what creation's fulfillment might mean. In fact, even though we may give primary attention to the issues surrounding origin, the questions about God, God's relationship to the world, and God's purpose or goal for creation may be the more significant issues the doctrine of creation addresses. These move us beyond curiosity about the past—or things "too lofty" for us to know—to the practical dynamics of our present and future life with God and the world.

The ancient habits of Western culture are not the only factor that has led us, in recent history, to focus our doctrine on origins. Some of the discussions about creation in the last century—especially between religious and scientific viewpoints—have gotten stuck on issues of origins and events of the past. And tragically, many people have been hurt as discussions turned into verbal attacks against people who disagree. As we look at the way God's people in the Old Testament, New Testament, and history of Christianity have interacted with their surrounding cultures, hopefully we can see how believers today can engage with our own scientific age. Also, we can hopefully see from the witness of Scripture and the Christian tradition what the doctrine of creation means for the present and future. Indeed, the doctrine of creation is one area of biblical teaching with direct implications for Christian action amid the flood of news about animal extinction and habitat loss, pollution from human-created waste, and climate change.[16]

The Shape of the Book

There are several general aims of this book. The first is to look at the many facets of the doctrine of creation. This includes not only dimensions of the who, what, and why of creation but also the complexity that Scripture teaches us about living in the world.

Second, the doctrine of creation had practical implications from the time God's people first started writing about it. In the various chapters, we will pick up ways that this doctrine matters for everyday living.

---

16. The doctrine of creation is not the only thing Christians affirm that helps us think about a Christian response to environmental issues. Michael Lodahl and April Maskiewicz teach about our environmental responsibilities out of Christianity's doctrine of the incarnation in *Renewal in Love: Living Holy Lives in God's Good Creation* (Kansas City, MO: Beacon Hill Press of Kansas City, 2014).

The last aim is to explore the history of viewpoints about creation. To some degree, this history provides the outline for the book. As we move through the viewpoints, our theology of creation and its everyday implications will rise to the surface.

Chapter 2 will take us into the ancient context in which God's people were first reflecting on the nature and character of God.

Chapters 3 and 4 examine Genesis 1, which has been highly significant in the history of theological reflection.

Chapter 5 explores other Old Testament teachings on the doctrine of creation.

Chapter 6 turns to New Testament teachings about creation.

Chapter 7 continues to examine the history of Christians wrestling with the doctrine of creation in light of the challenges they faced.

The final chapter takes us to our current context in presenting creation out of nothing in a Trinitarian way. It helps us think through creaturely agency and offers some practical implications for believers.

TWO

Ancient Outlooks

We are surrounded with stories. In many ways, who we are is shaped by stories. Each of us is a unique intersection of unfolding stories. Our identity can only be understood in that intersection. Families, for instance, have stories, and family gatherings can be opportunities to tell our stories together.

One Christmas I had the chance to attend the gathering of all my grandmother's siblings. The entertainment that day was listening to my grandmother's generation tell the stories of their childhood—what they did together (or to one another!), the way their parents ran their home, or decisions they each made that shaped their lives. While these were *their* stories, they also provided context for my own story; they gave meaning to what I had experienced as being part of this family. Through the years, from different branches of my family, I have heard stories of faith, perseverance, fidelity, and sacrifice. While the stories sound extraordinary to me, I have learned from the outlook of my elders that such things are not spectacular or heroic; they are what is required of us, expected, and simply what kind of people we are. For this family, these stories represent *normal*. They see no reason to feel pride or be praised for living the only way they know how. To be anything different would be the thing that would stick out. The out-of-the-ordinary stories in the family history are the ones we struggle to make sense of together. The normal (yet exemplary) stories are taken for granted; there is nothing to figure out. For example, it is entirely normal that a couple stays faithfully married until death, even through severe life circumstances. What we might struggle to make sense of is the person who broke away from the family.

Humans are more complex than just our families' stories. Our schools, churches, communities, clubs, workplaces, friend groups, media surroundings, and nations all tell stories too. These various places of influence and belonging provide the stories that help frame our sense of who we are, what is *normal* for us, our ideals, and our desires. We are shaped at the intersection of these (sometimes conflicting) stories.[1] We can communicate to others who we are and what we believe by telling stories, including stories about our dreams and what we seek to accomplish.

Stories—and telling them—are not new to humankind. Ancient people also had stories that shaped them. They belonged to families, broader social-political groups, and religious environments. We can get into their different cultures and life processes by listening to their stories. We can see what was normal and what broke the mold. In this chapter, we want to see what was normal for the groups who surrounded Israel. We will see how drastically Abraham's world changed when God called him to leave his roots. By looking at the stories that shaped the cultural imaginations of different ancient people, we will be able to see how Israel's beliefs (that may not seem extraordinary to us because we are familiar with them) were quite remarkable. Knowing Israel's surroundings brings Israel's beliefs into focus. We can get to know the broader ancient con-

---

1. For example, it is hard to reconcile stories that praise and uplift ideas of the American dream of upward mobility with the narrative of Christ's downward movement best expressed in Philippians 2. These two stories move in opposite directions.

text by following the life of Abraham and learning how he would have experienced various stories of ancient peoples.

Abraham's Roots

How readily do seventy-five-year-old men change their stories and uproot their lives? The Bible does not give us every detail of Abraham's early years. Yet, from what we do know, it indicates how drastically Abraham's world changed when God called him. God even changed Abraham's name from Abram, which is what it had been most of his life.

Abram was born "in Ur of the Chaldeans" (Gen. 11:28). The detail about Ur being "of the Chaldeans" is noteworthy since, in Abraham's time period, this region would not yet have been called by the name Israel knew later as Chaldea. The first time the area around Ur was called Chaldea was roughly one thousand years after the time when Abraham would have lived there. The clarification "of the Chaldeans" better fits the time period of Israel's exile in the sixth century BCE, supporting the view of those scholars who suggest that Genesis was written and/or edited at the time of Israel's exile or later.[2] Ur was a key port city at the southeast end of Mesopotamia, where the Euphrates River used to empty into the Persian Gulf. This region of Mesopotamia, also known as the Fertile Crescent, served as a center for civilization and innovation—for example, they literally invented the wheel![3] The region's resources sustained a series of different empires over thousands of years.

---

2. See "Chaldea: Ancient State, Middle East," *Encyclopaedia Britannica*, https://www.britannica.com/place/Chaldea; and "Ancient Jewish History: The Chaldeans (612–539 BCE)," Jewish Virtual Library, https://www.jewishvirtuallibrary.org/the-chaldeans-612-539bce.

3. Geoffrey P. Dobson, *A Chaos of Delight: Science, Religion and Myth and the Shaping of Western Thought* (London: Equinox, 2005), 25. "The Sumerians invented writing; they possessed the most amazing creation and cosmological myths; they invented the wheel, plough and ox-cart; they invented the 60-minute division of the hour, 60-second division of the minute and 360 parts to a

By Abram's time, the region had already had a proud history of various Sumerian and Akkadian dynasties, with their accompanying political, religious, and economic practices.[4]

Thanks to the Sumerians inventing cuneiform—one of the earliest forms of writing dating back to 3200 BCE—we can read about the religious beliefs from Abram's first seventy-five years.[5] It was common in his culture to believe different parts of the world were connected to different gods. For instance, the realms of the heavens, earth, or waters were often connected to the most primal gods, like the god An (or Anu) being the god above,[6] Enlil having the domain of the air and land,[7] and Enki being connected with waters and/or the realm under the earth.[8] These associations blurred people's understanding of whether the elements of the world themselves were the deity or if the deity inhabited that realm. In general, the Sumerians imagined the world as being filled with or connected to deities. In the Sumerian stories of creation, the primal gods (i.e., elements) gave birth to more gods, which meant

---

circle to map their skies; they practiced metallurgy and experimented with the arts and crafts" (Dobson, 25).

4. Figuring out when Abraham lived is difficult. Some scholars put his life later (2000–1800 BC), which would mean he was born when the last Sumerian dynasty had fallen and the Assyrian empire was on the rise.

5. "The World's Oldest Writing," *Archaeology* (May/June 2016), https://www.archaeology.org/issues/213-1605/features/4326-cuneiform-the-world-s-oldest-writing. For some of this religious history, see Joshua J. Mark, "Mesopotamian Religion," *Ancient History Encyclopedia*, https://www.ancient.eu/Mesopotamian_Religion/. See also this summary of creation beliefs by Samuel Noah Kramer in the second chapter of *Sumerian Mythology: A Study of Spiritual and Literary Achievement in the Third Millennium B.C.* (New York: Harper & Row, 1961): http://www.sacred-texts.com/ane/sum/sum07.htm. Here is a catalogue of Sumerian mythologies: http://etcsl.orinst.ox.ac.uk/catalogue/catalogue1.htm.

6. Kathryn Stevens, "An/Anu (god)," Ancient Mesopotamian Gods and Goddesses, http://oracc.museum.upenn.edu/amgg/listofdeities/an/index.html.

7. Adam Stone, "Enlil/Ellil (god)," Ancient Mesopotamian Gods and Goddesses, http://oracc.museum.upenn.edu/amgg/listofdeities/enlil/index.html.

8. Ruth Horry, "Enki/Ea (god)," Ancient Mesopotamian Gods and Goddesses, http://oracc.museum.upenn.edu/amgg/listofdeities/enki/index.html.

the addition of new parts in the world. The new gods were associated with the new parts of the world (like the moon or sun), or governed facets of life in the world (like love and war). Thus, everything about the physical world and things a person could experience in life was connected with divine beings.[9] There was no such thing as a "natural" world into which the gods sometimes interjected. Rather, everything was itself divine or the result of divine action; all heavenly or earthly events "were only signs of the deity's activity (sometimes favorable, sometimes not)."[10] People believed they operated within divine spaces and activities, and their worship was as much to keep peace with the gods as it was to give proper respect.

Each Sumerian city served as a center of worship for one of the gods, who was that city's patron deity. Abram's hometown of Ur was the center for worshiping the very high-ranking god Nanna, the moon god. In the heart of Ur, during the height of its power, a towering ziggurat was built in honor of Nanna. Nanna's greatness came with being the firstborn son of the high gods Enlil and Ninlil. According to one legend, Enlil and Ninlil were the two gods who not only arranged the heavens, earth, and underworld but also

---

9. While K. L. Noll is specifically describing Canaanite religion in the following quotation, it is a helpful clarification about Mesopotamian, Canaanite, and Egyptian religions: "The four ranks in human society—royal, noble, peasant, and slave—were mirrored by four tiers of gods. . . . At the top stood the divine patron and sometimes his spouse. In the second rank were the cosmic gods, who ruled aspects of the natural realm such as the storms that fertilized the land, the lights in the sky, the endlessly chaotic sea, the vast earth, and the eternal underworld. On the third level were the gods who assisted with practical aspects of daily life, such as gods of craftsmanship, gods of childbearing, and the family ancestors who had become gods after death. The lowest rank of the gods, corresponding to slaves in human society, were the messengers." (Noll, "Canaanite Religion," *Religion Compass* 1/1 (2007): 61–92, https://people.brandonu.ca/nollk/canaanite-religion/). In biblical theology the middle two tiers of gods are eliminated, along with divinizing the elements of the cosmos.

10. John H. Walton, *The Lost World of Genesis One: Ancient Cosmology and the Origins Debate* (Downers Grove, IL: IVP Academic, 2009), 20.

How readily do seventy-five-year-old men change their stories and uproot their lives?

gave birth to the main gods who ruled in those realms, like Nanna—their eldest—who ruled the top realm, the heavens.[11] In the cosmic order, Nanna the moon god (night/dark) was then the father of the sun god, Utu (day/light).[12]

It made sense that Nanna, as firstborn son, was considered the patron deity of Ur, a key center of power. The port city had long been essential to the control of its area; it was a hub of culture, trade, and politics. Ur itself became the capital city for the last Sumerian dynasty, before Mesopotamia's transition to the Assyrian era (in 2004 BCE). The whole of Ur's identity—its politics, religion, and economy—revolved around its claimed connection to Nanna. Interestingly for Abram's family, the moon god was sometimes depicted as a bull and was considered to be the protector of shepherds.[13]

Abram's hometown had prestige. Living there undoubtedly would have shaped his own identity and perspective, not to mention his first language was likely either Akkadian or Sumerian, Mesopotamia's principle languages. Abram lived in Ur long enough for his father, Terah, to have two more sons, Nahor and Haran, and for Abram's brother Haran to have a daughter reach marrying age (Gen. 11:28–29).

In the sparse details of Abram's early years, Genesis offers a piercing fact about his brother: "While his father Terah was still alive, Haran died in Ur of the Chaldeans, in the land of his birth" (v. 28). This tragedy is coupled with Abram's wife, Sarai (later named Sarah), not being

---

11. Here is one Sumerian account of Enlil and Ninlil, in which Nanna is called Suen: http://etcsl.orinst.ox.ac.uk/section1/tr121.htm. While Nanna ruled from above the earth, Nanna's three brother gods were responsible for irrigating the land and governing the underworld. See Adam Stone, "Nanna/Suen/Sin (god)," Ancient Mesopotamian Gods and Goddesses, http://oracc.museum.upenn.edu/amgg/listofdeities/nannasuen/.

12. Joshua J. Mark, "Nanna," World History Encyclopedia, https://www.worldhistory.org/Nanna/.

13. Stone, "Nanna/Suen/Sin (god)."

able to bear children (v. 30). Terah reacted to these difficult circumstances by taking Lot, the son of his dead son, his eldest son, Abram, and Abram's wife, Sarai, who could not have a son, and leaving Ur (v. 31). It did not matter that Terah could have been over a hundred years old (v. 26). When he set out, Terah's intention was to have a complete change, to go to the land of Canaan, the Semitic peoples to the west. This would have disrupted all their life stories—a change of home, friends, political structures, culture, religion, and language. While he made it more than half the distance by traveling up the length of the Euphrates River, Terah did not quite make half the change he intended. He stayed within the boundaries of Mesopotamia. Even more, by settling in Harran (v. 31), he was settling in the second-most important center of worship for the moon god Nanna. Perhaps his breaking point with his patron god had healed by the time he made it to Harran, or he found during the journey that he could not break with Nanna after all. Harran, a city of the god Nanna and kindred city to Ur, is where Terah died at the age of 205 (v. 32).[14]

New Stories

Abram finished the journey his father started. For the first time in this family's story, God spoke. Hearing from a deity who was not in Abram's stories would have been a disruption to Abram's beliefs; this was a new, foreign story for him. This new deity (God) commanded Abram to go on to Canaan (Gen. 12:1). "He took his wife Sarai, his nephew Lot, all the possessions they had accumulated and the people they had acquired in Harran, and they set out for

---

14. It would be entirely speculative to guess which household gods Jacob's uncle Laban served (Gen. 31:17–35; see 35:1–5). As a shepherd, Laban may have thought, as other shepherds did, that Nanna looked out for him. Nanna could have been among the household gods Rachel stole from her father (Gen. 31:19).

the land of Canaan, and they arrived there" (v. 5). Since there was a famine going on in Canaan, his Mesopotamian caravan continued on through Canaan and down to Egypt (v. 10). While in Egypt, Sarai lived in Pharaoh's palace, and Abram had direct interaction with officials at the highest levels of Egyptian society (vv. 15–16). For lifelong Mesopotamians, this would have been a fancy introduction to Egyptian culture.

Egypt was another long-standing, dominant center of culture in the ancient world. They too connected their gods with facets of the natural world—water, air, sun, and the like. Even with all the religious diversity in Egypt between cities and time periods, it was fairly common among Egyptians to view the world as having begun with a primal water, out of which emerged the first god and a disk of land.[15] Their creation stories then multiply out the number of gods and various features of the world.

Egypt's stories of creation and the cosmic order sometimes contained dramatic moments—like one god's search for other missing gods, or political scheming among gods. However, for the most part, the Egyptians lived in an environment that was fairly predictable. Each day the sun moved from one horizon to the other; it disappeared below the horizon each evening into the primordial underworld and was reborn the next morning into the cosmic order above the horizon. Each year the Nile River rose up over its banks, deposited nutrient topsoil, then receded again.[16] All life was supported by the Nile's calm dependability. Their

---

15. For a quick overview of some different Egyptian beliefs, see "5 Egyptian Mythology Creation Stories Animated," https://www.youtube.com/watch?v=wHdg8yENKJk; see also "Ancient Egyptian Creation Myth," https://www.youtube.com/watch?v=t4wd0wNHYgA.

16. Dobson, *A Chaos of Delight*: "Every year for over ten thousand years it has overflowed its banks from the high summer monsoon rainfalls in Ethiopia and the East African Plateau" (56). As a result of the rains, "the water level began to rise in late June or early July (beginning at the summer solstice), reached its

creation stories were relatively harmonious in narrating the emergence of the world and the gods from primal waters. In Abram's Sumerian creation narratives, the gods were more prone to deceive one another, struggle among themselves for superiority, and at times even battle one another to the death. Their river systems were less predictable than the Nile. The unpredictable floods of the Tigris and Euphrates were known to take away what they had at first given.[17] In Egypt, Abram was hearing stories that projected a different sense of what was normal in this world of the gods.

Abram was sent away from Egypt with livestock and riches (Gen. 12:20–13:2). He was finally able to live in Canaan, and God made a promise to Abram that the land would be his (13:14–17). However, life in Canaan confronted him with a third set of political dynamics and religious beliefs. Politically—rather than having any central leadership over the region, like in Mesopotamia or Egypt—Canaan had many smaller ethnic groups, each under its own king (see, for example, Gen. 14:1–24). Canaan's religious stories contain names mentioned in the Old Testament, like the head god El and his consort Asherah, who together had seventy children, including Baal (who became ruler), Anat, Molech, and Astarte.[18] In the surviving Canaanite cre-

---

maximum at Cairo toward the end of September and subsided in November" (56).

17. See H. and H. A. Frankfort, "The Emancipation of Thought from Myth," *The Intellectual Adventure of Ancient Man* (Chicago: University of Chicago Press, 1977), 364f.; Thorkild Jacobsen, "Mesopotamia: The Cosmos as a State," *The Intellectual Adventure of Ancient Man* (Chicago: University of Chicago Press, 1977), 171f.

18. "Canaanite Gods and Goddesses," American Bible Society, http://bibleresources.americanbible.org/resource/canaanite-gods-and-goddesses; "Canaanite Religion," New World Encyclopedia, http://www.newworldencyclopedia.org/entry/Canaanite_Religion. Some of the scholarship comparing Canaanite beliefs to the beliefs about God among Israelites can be disturbing to modern Christians, but it need not destroy our appreciation for the biblical witness and what God taught the Israelites about who God is. Here are examples of different types of comparative studies: Joseph Lam, "Biblical Creation in its Ancient Near

ation accounts, we find multiple views about how creation happened—such as creation by a god speaking, sculpting things out of clay, or procreation. In some accounts, in order to work out the hierarchy between gods, primordial battles were fought between deities. The battle would determine who could be the creator.

Israel's Context

Even with all the local differences Abram experienced across the ancient world, there were also many similarities. Each culture imagined the world to consist of three levels: the heavens, the earth, and under the earth. The heavens consisted of a solid dome (or deity) over their heads, spanning from one horizon to the other; it served to hold up waters that are suspended in the sky. In addition, the heavenly canopy above held the sun, moon, and stars. These cultures had no idea that rain did not come from waters held up in the sky by the dome (Gen. 7:11; 8:2), or that the sun, moon, and stars were at different distances and very far away. The second level was the land on which they lived; the land itself was held up over the more primal underworld by pillars, or foundations.[19] The third level was an underworld (often a watery abyss) beneath the land (see Jon. 2:3–6). Exodus 20:4, for example, names each of the three tiers in this ancient perspective, in order from top to

---

Eastern Context," *BioLogos* (April 1, 2010), https://biologos.org/resources/scholarly-articles/the-biblical-creation-in-its-ancient-near-eastern-context; Richard S. Hess and David Tashio Tsumura, eds., *I Studied Inscriptions from before the Flood: Ancient Near Eastern, Literary, and Linguistic Approaches to Genesis 1–11* (Winona Lake, IN: Eisenbrauns, 1994); Jed Robinson, "The God of the Patriarchs and the Ugaritic Texts: A Shared Religious and Cultural Identity," *Studia Antiqua* 8.1 (2010): 25–33, https://scholarsarchive.byu.edu/studiaantiqua/vol8/iss1/4/?utm_source=scholarsarchive.byu.edu%2Fstudiaantiqua%2Fvol8%2Fiss1%2F4&utm_medium=PDF&utm_campaign=PDFCoverPages); K. L. Noll, "Canaanite Religion," https://people.brandonu.ca/nollk/canaanite-religion/.

19. "Pillars of the Earth," *Encyclopedia of the Bible,* Bible Gateway, https://www.biblegateway.com/resources/encyclopedia-of-the-bible/Pillars-Earth.

bottom: "You shall not make for yourself an image in the form of anything in heaven above or on the earth beneath or in the waters below."

In all of the ancient Near Eastern origin stories, there was some type of primal material (usually water). That primal material could be either a divine being or simply the substance out of which the first god formed himself. Then the other gods or elements emerged to form the hierarchical structure of the cosmos as they imagined it. The connection of gods with each element or part of the world, as well as with each life function, meant that all features of existence were embedded in divinity. The cosmos was not thought of as *nature*, or following *natural* processes. Some type of agency was involved in everything.

The Old Testament testifies to the reality that Abraham and Sarah, their daughter-in-law, Rebekah (Isaac's wife), and their grandson Jacob's wives all came out of the cultural background of Mesopotamia. Rebekah, the sister of Laban, was an Aramean from Paddan Aram (Gen. 25:20); this identifies her with the area of Mesopotamia around Harran, a center for worship of Nanna. Laban is also identified as Aramean four times in Genesis (25:20; 28:5; 31:20, 24). These consistent identifications point to their Mesopotamian cultural and religious background. Others who left Paddan Aram with Jacob and his family had gods with them; Jacob told them all to bury their gods and their cultural-religious markings when they got to Canaan (35:1–5). Abraham, Isaac, and Jacob remained connected to people from their family's Mesopotamian origin, even generations after God commanded Abram, "Go from your country, your people and your father's household to the land I will show you" (12:1).

Abram and Sarai lived for a time in Egypt, and Hagar, who became their servant, was Egyptian. Even after coming out of Mesopotamia and Egypt, the family lived in Canaan among people with beliefs related to those from which they had come. Throughout their long history in the land of Canaan, the Israelites struggled to separate from the beliefs and practices of the people around them, which is why the Bible tells stories about them following Baal, trusting Asherah for fertility, or sacrificing to Canaanite gods like Molech. In every phase of their history, they interacted with these long-standing religious traditions. Abram and Sarai came from Mesopotamia. Their descendants were enslaved in Egypt for more than four hundred years. The Israelites lived around other people in Canaan. The land of Canaan itself was the crossroad between the east, west, north, and south of the ancient Near Eastern peoples. They were taken back into Mesopotamia under Babylonian captivity. In short, Israel was well informed of their neighbors' perspectives.

It should not surprise us, then, that Israel's own writings—Christianity's Old Testament—assume that the world has the same three-tiered structure that all ancient people thought it did. That was the thinking of the ancient Near East at that time, and Israel's writings reflect it. Perhaps more stirring, though, is that the various accounts of creation in the Old Testament echo details found across ancient Near Eastern writings, from Egypt in the west to Mesopotamia in the east. Hear this clearly, though: it is not that Israel copied sentences out of those other mythologies and cobbled them together into their own hybrid story. Rather, the primal starting point, the sequence of what gets made, the methods for making things, and the structure of the world are comparable to ancient teachings on creation. The fact that our Scriptures resonate with the context in which they were written should not alarm us. In fact, that resonance is precisely what would have made Israel's writings an appropriate and powerful message. They are understandable.

By paying careful attention to what is *different* in Israel's writings, even as they cover common ideas in their context, we can see what they are saying about God and creation. For instance, instead of saying *how* God was created or emerged, Genesis 1 starts with God already existing. Furthermore, God is not made out of the same substance as the primal waters or any part of the world. God's existence and substance are distinct from creation. As God's interaction with the primal waters moves forward in a familiar pattern to other ancient texts, new gods do not enter the narrative. There is only ever the one God. Also, the things made are not divine beings, or made out of the substance either of God or of any other gods. Creation is one kind of substance, and divinity (God) is an entirely distinct nature. In short, no matter how many similarities there are between the creation story in the Bible and the creation myths told by Israel's neighbors, Genesis is ultimately making profoundly different claims. The Bible's creation story and the other ancient creation myths do not have the same markers for what is considered *normal*. Even the character of various divine beings is different. For example, the brutality and selfishness that is a common theme in one god's stories is absent in the love and care attributed to Israel's God. The unique claims in Israel's writings are what we need to explore. The following chapters will dive into the ancient imagination and see what Israel had to say about God and creation. We will see how much the thinking of Abraham's descendants changed from their surrounding background.

THREE

Genesis 1
Beginning

Perhaps we should start with honesty. Genesis 1 (by which we usually mean Genesis 1:1–2:3) has been a battleground. Fellow Christians have attacked one another over interpretations of this text. We have treated one another hurtfully and unlovingly.

For some readers, even wading into this chapter raises anxiety levels. They hardly feel they can trust how other believers will respond to their positions. Without clear signals, they do not know if they will be treated as an ally or an enemy. Given our history, avoidance may seem like the safest route. Some may want to retreat into trenches where they feel secure among like-minded people. Perhaps others are so tired of Genesis 1 debates, they can hardly bear to read one more position on the topic; they have quit the field. They are so over it that the effort to read any further requires more energy than they can muster. There may be a handful who still believe that battling over certain interpretations of Genesis 1 is our Christian duty—even if that means battling fellow Christians. I may be wrong, but it seems this last group is shrinking in number as more Christians realize that focusing on our witness and being the hands and feet of Christ is the church's foremost priority.

Bottom line, we must stop attacking each other. We must stop treating each other as enemies. No matter any differences of perspective we have, we must love each other. I pray we can all quit the battlefield together. The integrity of the message of Christ demands our unity in love: as Christ prayed, "Then the world will know that you sent me and have loved them even as you have loved me" (John 17:23). And, if Genesis 1 has a consistent message, it is one of care for our neighbor. It is tragic to fight over a text that teaches the opposite of warfare and domination. Through what follows, I hope to open sincere, loving dialogue about this text.

The goal of this chapter is to step back and find our bearings. Archaeologists say that recovering cultural artifacts on the black market and having the chance to examine them is nice. It is better, however, if those artifacts had not been removed from their original location. So much information is lost when artifacts are looted from where they were. Archaeologists may never know the exact site where an item came from, how it was situated, what other items were found with it, its function or significance, and all the information each item could have helped us learn about that past culture. Context adds layers to our understanding about an item that it cannot tell us by itself.

We need to do the same thing with Genesis 1. We need to explore it in its context. In the previous chapter, we began to look at the context of the broader ancient Near East; we will remain mindful of that broader context as we look at Genesis 1. We will also look at Genesis 1 in the context of the whole book of Genesis, the Torah, and the Bible. Before diving into the bulk of the Genesis 1 narrative in the next chapter, we will take a focused look at the opening verses. This is part of understanding Genesis 1 in its biblical location and in relation to Israel's broader context.

We also need to think about influences from our own context. In the late 1800s, some suggestions that have become quite common were made for reading the first verses of Genesis 1, such as reading verse 2 as representing *chaos*, or anti-God forces. At the same time as those suggestions became common in teaching, some scholars were rejecting those same ideas as unsupportable. That conversation needs to be unpacked (some of which is done in the footnotes to keep the chapter moving). We will also need to explore what to do with this text and Christianity's doctrine of creation out of nothing. Tension between the text and Christianity's doctrine has created a long history of interpretations that try to resolve the tension.

In short, the goal of this chapter is to reflect on Genesis 1 in its context and how it introduces itself. Then we will be ready to look at its seven days in the next chapter.

Place in the Bible

If we imagine that the whole Bible is a single narrative, then we can think about its overall literary structure, along with the internal structure of its various parts. With that approach, Genesis 1 has the special privilege of standing at the beginning of the Bible. It sets the tone and introduces certain themes as it opens the arc of the biblical plot. That plot starts "in the beginning" (Gen. 1:1). There is no time further back or before the scope of the Bible's interest. It starts with God, who is the first and primary actor from the beginning to eternity.

The passage introduces itself as a narrative of "the heavens and the earth" (v. 1). This phrase is a merism, which is naming two things that together refer to an entirety. For example, in English, the phrase "head to toe" is a merism that means a person's whole body, nothing excluded. "The heavens and the earth" means *everything*, top to bottom. As the Nicene Creed says it, God is creator of "all there is, visible and invisible." It may not always come to mind that the heavens are as much part of God's creation as the earth, but this is a narrative about the beginning of everything except God, who has no beginning. The heavens (or the singular heaven) are not eternal. The heavens are *in* the world—a feature of God's creation.[1] By leading out with this text, Scripture boldly presents itself as the shared cosmic story of all space and time, and of the one God who governs it all. The Bible is far from a humble book; it is the story of everything!

Along with being first for the whole Bible, this passage is also first for the Torah—Israel's five books of the Law, Genesis through Deuteronomy. Though more than being *law* (or laws), these books lay out *life direction*. They are teaching, or instruction, for the way God's people are to conduct themselves through life. This is why these books are also called *halakhah*, "the path that one walks."[2] This way of thinking about the Torah, or Jewish law, as a way for walking makes sense with so much of these five books being stories. These narratives do not command or give laws as often as they teach through illustration. Genesis is a great example. Rather than always explaining what should be done or what the narratives mean, Genesis leaves readers to carefully reflect on its lessons—as irreducibly complex, subtle, or unspoken as those lessons may be.

Genesis 1, as life-directing Torah, has many indirect ways of teaching. For example, through its structural features, it highlights the idyllic unfolding of God's activities, which foster "a fully stable, life-sustaining, differentiated

---

1. Based on the rest of the Bible, we can define heaven "as 'the place in the world from which' God's action, insofar as it is an innerworldly action, originates" (Robert W. Jenson, *Systematic Theology, Volume 2: The Works of God* [Oxford: Oxford University Press, 1999], 120; Jenson's quotation is from Karl Barth). God's will is done in heaven, and we pray it will be done on earth as well (Matt. 6:10). Thus, heaven already enjoys what earth still awaits. "Heaven is the presence in creation of earth's final future" (Jenson, 126). The opening of heaven at Christ's baptism signals the good news that God's dominion has been and is coming on earth—to be fully enjoyed, without end, at Christ's return.

2. Tracey R. Rich, "Halakhah: Jewish Law," Judaism 101, http://www.jewfaq.org/halakhah.htm.

world."³ An indirect way it does this is through patterns of seven: "God 'saw' and pronounced creation 'good' seven times; 'earth' or 'land' (same word in Hebrew) appears twenty-one times; 'God' is repeated thirty-five times. The number seven, or multiples thereof, also crops up within certain discrete passages: Genesis 1:1 consists of seven words; 1:2 features fourteen words; Genesis 2:1–3 renders a word count of thirty-five. In fact, the total word count of the narrative proper (1:1–2:3) is 469 in Hebrew (7 x 67)."⁴ Even though the text does not outright say it, there is no hostility between God and this unfolding world; from first to last, the whole narrative is framed in the sweetness of sevens. This depiction of the relationship between God and creation opens the Torah.

Genesis 1 not only stands first—it also stands apart. The next section starts in Genesis 2:4 with the introductory formula *toledot*: "this is the story of . . ." or, "this is what became of . . .".⁵ Genesis 2:4 takes up the story of the heavens

---

3. William P. Brown, *The Seven Pillars of Creation: The Bible, Science, and the Ecology of Wonder* (New York: Oxford University Press, 2010), 37.

4. Brown, *Seven Pillars*, 37.

5. D. Lyle Dabney, "The Nature of the Spirit," *The Work of the Spirit*, ed. Michael Welker (Grand Rapids: Eerdmans, 2006), 75. There are challenges with what to make of the eleven *toledot* statements in Genesis (Gen. 2:4; 5:1; 6:9; 10:1; 11:10, 27; 25:12, 19; 36:1, 9; 37:2); see Marten H. Woudstra, "The Toledot of the Book of Genesis and Their Redemptive-Historical Significance," *Calvin Theological Journal* 5 (1970): 188, https://faculty.gordon.edu/hu/bi/ted_hildebrandt/otesources/01-genesis/text/articles-books/woudstra_gentoledot_ctj.pdf. Joseph Coleson does not agree with a strong division between the narratives of Genesis 1 and 2. In his commentary on Genesis 1–11, Coleson says chapter 2 is the second episode in a two-part drama. Genesis 2:4 is a bit like "snippets of scenes from the first part, refreshing the viewer's memory and setting up the action to come" (Coleson, *Genesis 1–11*, New Beacon Bible Commentary [Kansas City, MO: Beacon Hill Press of Kansas City, 2012], 80). Though it starts the next unit, verse 4 binds this new unit with Genesis 1. Verse 4 has the seventh use of *bara* ("create") that is missing from Genesis 1, even while it starts the narrative about what became of the heavens and the earth, especially humankind within it (see Coleson, *Genesis 1–11*, 80–84). Coleson outright rejects splitting verse 4 in half as the NRSV, NLT, and JPS do (82).

and the earth. Genesis 1 is preliminary. Like a preface or prologue, it lies behind and before any story of Scripture.[6] There are interesting options of what it might mean for chapter 1 if it stands before any stories that emerge after this baseline orienting text.[7] One option is how St. Irenaeus of Lyon (AD 130–202) read it. He took Genesis 1 to be a miniature version of the whole story of the Bible. Since creation awaits the true Sabbath rest (day 7), we are still in day 6. The entire history of animals and humans on the planet—including the history of sin and salvation—has been taking place in this sixth day. Day 7 will come when Christ returns and reigns forever.

A second option is to think of the chapter as a liturgical text. Some ancient Near Eastern cultures read their creation stories at an annual new-year festival, like Babylon's Akitu festival. Just as the Egyptians could imagine the sun to be reborn each morning it came up over the horizon, Israel's various neighbors could imagine the land being created anew each spring after the soaking floods and rains. Their gods did the work of creation in a year-by-year cycle. We do not have record, however, that Israel used Genesis 1 in an annual festival like their neighbors used their texts. Also, Genesis 1 itself is a one-week cycle of work and rest that Israel was to follow at all times (e.g., Exod. 16:23–29; 20:8–11; 31:12–17). Even so, this idea of Genesis 1 as a liturgical text may not be entirely wrong. The Torah could be

---

6. See Richard J. Clifford, *Creation Accounts in the Ancient Near East and in the Bible* (New York: Catholic Biblical Association, 1994), 143. I thank Alex Varughese and Ben Boeckel for their helpful input on the *toledot* formula and issues of the literary structure of Genesis. See Ben Boeckel's excursus on *toledot* in *Covenant and Its Use in the Enneateuch: A Form-Critical Investigation* (PhD diss., Southern Methodist University, 2016), 100–105. On the preliminary nature of the larger unit of Genesis 1–11, see Clifford, *Creation Accounts*, 143–49. For a helpful diagram looking at the structure of Genesis on the basis of the main male and female characters see David W. Cotter, *Genesis, Berit Olam: Studies in Hebrew Narrative & Poetry* (Collegeville, MN: The Liturgical Press, 2003), 79–82.

7. Woudstra, "The Toledot of the Book of Genesis," 188.

opening—appropriately—with a text that takes us into the glorification of our Creator (like Psalm 104). All things in Genesis 1, including humankind, are joined in their common vocation of glorifying their Creator.[8]

A third option, like the second, is not to make Genesis 1 a yearly occurrence or figure out where we are in its sequence of days. If it is the preface or condition for understanding all that follows, it can be an overarching statement about what life in God's creation is meant to be at all times. As Torah, it can be a teaching that calibrates our understanding about God and God's intentions for the world's functioning. It permeates all time: our whole sense of life's purpose and meaning. After setting a baseline regarding God's intentions for creation, the rest of Genesis helps introduce us to dynamics at work in the world—movements toward or away from God's purposes.

So here is what is being suggested: First, as Torah, this chapter frames the entirety of life for God's creation, just as Israel's religious practices framed their day-to-day life in Canaan. It is profound that this text is not just about Israel. It is about the one Redeemer-Creator-Ruler of all creation and peoples.[9] God is creation's provision. All life

---

8. I thank Alex Varughese for pointing out the option of praise. As he also noted in private correspondence (March 2019), it would not be out of character within Israel to connect praises of God as Creator with praises for being the Giver of Torah. In Psalm 19, "the first part (vv. 1–6) is praise of the Creator, and the second part (vv. 7–13) is praise of the Creator who gave the law to Israel; it concludes with a doxological statement (v. 14)" (Varughese, private correspondence). See also Michael Lodahl, *All Things Necessary to Our Salvation*, Monograph Series, Number Four (San Diego: Point Loma Press, 2004), 38–46, https://www.pointloma.edu/centers-institutes/wesleyan-center/point-loma-press. Lodahl notes a history in Wesleyan-Holiness scholarship of seeing Genesis 1 as a "hymn of creation" (38–39).

9. Indeed, the narrative of Genesis is about the heavens and the earth, the common human story, and various people groups. Even with the turn to Abraham and Sarah, God's intention was to bless all nations through them (Genesis 12:1-3). Other people of the world were not forgotten or written out of this narrative. Genesis remains their story too, since God is also their Ruler-Creator and

in the world depends on God's presence and activity. God is actively present in and through all, just as the whole of space and time are located in God's un-boundedness. Second, Genesis 1 starts the Torah by organizing the whole life of creation toward the praise and glorification of God. In short, Genesis 1 is Torah for living in God's creation at all times. "The earth is filled with your love, Lord; teach me your decrees" (Ps. 119:64).

Where to Begin?

In ancient Near East creation narratives, there were two ways to describe the starting conditions. One way was through negation: "before there was x," or, "when there was no x."[10] Here are some examples.

Egyptian

"Not existed heaven, not existed earth, not had been created the things of the earth, (i.e., plants) and creeping things in place that; I raised up them from out of Nu (i.e., the primeval abyss of water) from a state of inactivity. Not found I a place I could stand wherein."[11]

---

life purpose. God works as Redeemer of all humankind and creation through the covenant people (Lodahl and Maskiewicz, *Renewal in Love*). In short, the life of Israel is framed in religious imagination, as the life of all creation is framed in Genesis 1 imagination—even as the life of Israel is inseparably interwoven with the story of all creation and peoples.

10. See Clifford, *Creation Accounts*, 101–103. Claus Westermann has also noted this ancient way of narrating creation, by first describing "when there was not yet." Our present "state and all that is taken for granted with it is, as it were, abolished for a moment; the present and apparently permanent state of the world is taken back to a moment when an event is taking place in which the present state is in the process of becoming." The primeval starting point is a "not yet" condition (Westermann, *Genesis 1–11: A Commentary*, trans. John J. Scullion, SJ [Minneapolis: Augsburg Publishing House, 1984], 43).

11. Barbara C. Sproul, *Primal Myths: Creating the World* (San Francisco: Harper & Row, 1979), 81f.

Sumerian

"Earth was in darkness, the lower world was [invi]sible; the waters did not flow through the opening (in the earth), nothing was produced, on the vast earth the furrow had not been made. The high priest of Enlil did not exist. The rites of purification were not carried out . . . heaven was not adorned, she did not proclaim. . . . Heaven and earth were joined to each other (forming) a unit."[12]

Genesis 2:5-6

"Now no shrub had yet appeared on the earth and no plant had yet sprung up, for the LORD God had not sent rain on the earth and there was no one to work the ground, but streams came up from the earth and watered the whole surface of the ground."

The second way of describing the primal starting conditions—and a closer fit to Genesis 1—was as a watery state, and sometimes darkness was included.[13] Notice that this second way of starting with waters and darkness is sometimes blended with the first way of negation. The Egyptian example above uses negation while everything is raised out of the primal waters. In the Babylonian example below, there are the male and female waters of Apsu and Mummu-Tiamat, even while there is a description of all that is not.

Babylonian

"When on high the heaven had not been named, firm ground below had not been called by name, naught but primordial Apsu, their begetter, (and) Mummu-Tiamat, she who bore them all, their waters commingling as a single

---

12. Walton, *The Lost World of Genesis One*, 52.
13. The old Sumerian traditions started with waters, "represented as the goddess Nammu (or Namma)." The goddess Nammu was "the mother, who gave birth to heaven and earth" (Dobson, *A Chaos of Delight*, 32).

body; no reed hut had been matted, no marsh land had appeared, when no gods whatever had been brought into being, uncalled by name, their destinies undetermined—then it was that the gods were formed within them."[14]

Egyptian

"In the beginning, before there was any land of Egypt, all was darkness, and there was nothing but a great waste of water called Nun."[15]

Genesis 1:2

"And the earth was a waste and desolate emptiness, and darkness was over the face of the deep, and the Spirit of God was hovering over the face of the waters" (NASB, following alternate translations in the footnotes).

As mentioned in the previous chapter, it is not as though the biblical authors plagiarized other cultures. Rather, they remain within ancient cultural assumptions about primal conditions and how to describe them, along with the general sequence and cosmic arrangement of what gets created. The key thing to note is where Israel's texts are *different* from the general thinking of their time. "The full implication of texts are known within and in contrast to their [ancient Near Eastern] environment."[16] Attention to

---

14. "The Babylonian Epic of Creation: 'When on High'," Academy for Ancient Texts, http://www.ancienttexts.org/library/mesopotamian/enuma.html.

15. "The Story of Re," Ancient Egypt: The Mythology, http://www.egyptianmyths.net/mythre.htm.

16. Hess, "One Hundred Fifty Years of Comparative Studies on Genesis 1–11: An Overview," *I Studied Inscriptions before the Flood*, 24. There have been poor examples of comparative studies between ancient Near Eastern cultures and texts through the years. In the late 1800s it was common to say the biblical creation narratives were directly based on other cultures' texts, or simply represented a next step in the development of ancient thinking. As early as 1926, Benno Landsberger was cautioning that assumptions were being made about there being a shared worldview among ancient Semitic cultures. In response to the unfounded assumptions, attention to nuances within individual cultures and languages developed among scholars, including scholars who began to

context helps bring into sharper focus what Israel believed about God and the world.

Introducing Itself

The book of Genesis begins each of its sections with an introductory statement. Genesis 1 follows this pattern by having a brief introductory statement of its own (seven words in Hebrew).[17] "In the beginning God created the heavens and the earth" (1:1). This is a general statement that summarizes what will be narrated in 1:2–2:3. That would give verse 1 the sense of, "This is the story of the beginning, when God created the heavens and the earth."[18] Since the Middle Ages, one option for translating verse 1 has been to make it a temporal clause that leads into the primal conditions described in verse 2. The NRSV follows

---

specialize in just one culture (Hess, 9f.). Sloppy, superficial comparisons became less tolerated among scholars of ancient Near East cultures, even while biblical scholars remained less careful (Hess, 18). In fact, in 1966 it was noted: "Old Testament scholarship has made only superficial use of ancient Near Eastern data. The main reasons, of course, are fairly obvious. Ancient . . . studies are both complex and highly specialized" (K. A. Kitchen, *Ancient Orient and Old Testament* [Downers Grove, IL: InterVarsity Press, 1966], 24; see pp. 17–27 to see some history of struggles in making comparisons and 28–32 for the development of standards in methodology). G. F. Hasel noted in a 1972 essay about Genesis 1: "In few other passages of the Bible have so many facile comparisons been made with ancient Near Eastern myths and so many far-reaching conclusions posited" (quoted in Hess, 19f.). Through the 1980s and 1990s, a generation of biblical scholarship began to note how different the biblical writings are from other ancient literature. This acknowledgment brought new levels of appreciation for what exactly the biblical authors were saying within, and in response to, their broader environment.

17. Coleson, *Genesis 1–11*, 41. Paul Copan and William Lane Craig offer an extensive argument for taking verse 1 as an independent sentence (*Creation out of Nothing: A Biblical, Philosophical, and Scientific Exploration* [Grand Rapids: Baker, 2004], 36–49). It should be noted they also suggest that Genesis 1 teaches creation out of nothing. Taking verse 1 as a statement of creation out of nothing is commonly rejected within scholarship.

18. See Andrew Mayer Hahn, *Tohu Va-Vohu: Matter, Nothingness and Non-being in Jewish Creation Theology*, PhD diss., Jewish Theological Seminary of America, 2002, 37.

this option: "In the beginning when God created the heavens and the earth, the earth was . . ."[19] Given that the whole passage tends to use shorter sentences and this seven-word sentence is followed by the fourteen-word sentence of verse 2, it makes sense to keep verse 1 a separate sentence. It is a statement introducing the topic of the whole passage. Some scholars even liken the first verse to a newspaper headline or photograph caption.

Then What Did "Create" Mean?

The word "create" (*bara*) appears in Genesis 1:1—as well as in 1:21, 27, and 2:3. We need to clarify the word "create" in the introductory statement of verse 1 in order to understand the character of the narrative that follows in Genesis 1:2–2:3. As a starting point, it is important to note that "create" (*bara*) is a special action for God alone. All fifty appearances of *bara* in the Old Testament are God's action.[20] We will see the significance of this as we look at what God's action does.

We have seen that ancient creation narratives open either by listing what is not yet and/or with a dark, watery condition. The process of *creating* typically unfolds as a series of actions that divide, or separate out, *new* features or conditions—what had not been the case before.[21] In Genesis 1 in particular, we can see that God's creative process includes speaking, seeing, separating, setting, naming, making, and blessing. Given this diverse list, in the work of creating, it is not enough that something is produced or

---

19. While this has been discussed among scholars, I side with those who argue for verse 1 as an independent sentence; see Westermann, *Genesis 1–11*, 95–97; Terrance Fretheim, "The Book of Genesis," *The New Interpreter's Bible* (Nashville: Abingdon Press, 1994), 342; Coleson, *Genesis 1–11*, 41.

20. Walton, *The Lost World of Genesis One*, 40.

21. Westermann, *Genesis 1–11*, 34; Fretheim, "The Book of Genesis," *NIB*, 342.

becomes distinguishable as a thing. *Bara* is not limited to or primarily about "producing and causing."²² In the focus of the narrative, *bara* has more to do with working out the function of the world than producing the material substance of the world. We can think of the concept of *bara* as *making a new situation that is to function according to divine purposes*.

Some new situations God "creates" in the Bible have nothing to do with producing materials—like "making [*bara*] a covenant" (Exod. 34:10), a condition (Jer. 31:22), or God's covenant people (Ezek. 21:30; Mal. 2:10). It is not that material objects do not come to exist in the Genesis 1 narrative; God makes light, lights, a dome, and other things. However, the details about where they come from, what they are made of, or how God makes them are not in the narrative. What is explained is what these things are made *for*.²³ We can see this functional emphasis of God's creative activity when we note that *bara* is never used in the Old Testament with "out of" in order to refer to what type of material something is made with, or with reference to a substance *out of* which it comes.²⁴

Certainly something new, or a new circumstance, is the result of creating. Yet material construction is not the focus of creating, nor is *coming into existence* sufficient to

---

22. Michael Welker, "What is Creation? Rereading Genesis 1 and 2," *Theology Today* 48.1 (Apr 1991): 64. Welker suggests we have wrongly limited our understanding of creation to "a process of being produced by a transcendent reality." Along with this, we have thought of our creaturely status as simply "absolute dependence upon this transcendent reality" (59). Yet, in Genesis 1 and 2, creation is not about production and causation. God's creative process includes many kinds of actions. This, Welker believes, needs to reframe our ideas about the relationship of our Creator to the created world (60–61). "Genesis 1 and 2 describe the entire creation as in many respects having its own activity, as being itself productive, as being itself causative" (61f.).

23. Coleson, *Genesis 1–11*, 38.

24. Westermann, *Genesis 1–11*, 108–9; Walton, *The Lost World of Genesis One*, 41–44; Fretheim, "The Book of Genesis," *NIB*, 342.

summarize what God's act of creation accomplishes. Any craftsperson can separate and arrange materials. To be *Creator* and do the work of *creation* is to have the capacity or authority to convey function or purpose for the heavens and the earth.[25] Function is illustrated in Genesis 2; it is "not good" for man to be alone; that circumstance is not working. Thus, God made woman. Yes, she was *formed* out of *his* rib/side and was bone of his bone and flesh of his flesh. However, she was to be ʿēzer kĕnegdô—"a power/strength corresponding/equal to him" or "a power/strength like him, corresponding to him, of the same kind or species, facing [or: opposite] him as [an] equal."[26] Her function (or relation in the world) is named when God makes her as a corrective to the "not good" situation.

To be Creator is to govern—by providing, preserving, overseeing, and establishing norms for creation's conduct. Only the Ruler-Creator can rightfully establish something's purpose. In God's creative governance, new circumstances are made; more importantly, a direction is introduced according to which creation is to operate. Creating extends purpose or function to each part and, thus, the character of shared life in the whole world. That collective functioning of all parts is creation's *economy*—or household norm.[27] Precedent for operating in this kingdom—this domain—resides with the Ruler, who has dominion.[28] Being Creator for

---

25. Walton, *The Lost World of Genesis One*, 43. See his chapter-long explanation, 38–46.

26. Coleson, *Genesis 1–11*, 102, 103. On the translation of "side" versus "rib," see Coleson, "The Human Race Completed—Commentary," *The Creation Mandate*, Wynkoop Center Bible Studies on Women in Ministry, http://whdl.org/en/browse/resources/9492.

27. "Economy" comes into English from the Greek word *oikonomos*—*oikos* ("household") and *nomos* ("law," "custom").

28. Jon D. Levenson has suggested that God is fighting to gain this dominion, and God's dominion is continually threatened in the Bible (see *Creation and the Persistence of Evil*). I have countered his position in my book *Creation and Chaos Talk: Charting a Way Forward*. Levenson's proposal does not fit texts like Psalm

doctrine of creation out of nothing is not found in the ancient world of Israel and "is foreign to Genesis 1."[32] It might create some discomfort, but we want to hear what Genesis 1 was saying in its historic context rather than making it fit a doctrine that came about hundreds of years later. As we will see, these first verses may yet be saying something akin to creation out of nothing, but it is working in an ancient Near Eastern context and communicating through the available methods to do it.

In creating, God is extending "a moral intention for other beings than himself."[33] Creating is less about God causing existence or manipulating cause-and-effect processes. For creation and creatures, it is a matter of hearing and obeying God's moral intention for the world—not once upon a time, but forever.[34] Those intentions define our purpose for being and our destiny.

---

tion. Even as Jews were translating their scriptures from Hebrew into Greek, there was no reason for them to abandon the idea of creation out of a primal condition. "Given the consensus among the Greek philosophers beginning with Thales (sixth century BCE) concerning preexistent material and the lack of unambiguous textual evidence asserting the contrary before the Common Era, it is hard to imagine the [Septuagint] expounding the doctrine of *creatio ex nihilo* [creation out of nothing]" (Brown, 32). Gerhard May offers a helpful summary in his book's foreword of what ideas are included in a doctrine of creation out of nothing and when we see those features arise; see May, *Creatio Ex Nihilo: The Doctrine of 'Creation out of Nothing' in Early Christian Thought*, trans. A. S. Worrall (Edinburgh: T&T Clark, 1994), xi–xiv.

32. Westermann, *Genesis 1–11*, 109.

33. Jenson, *Systematic Theology, Volume 2*, 8. This way of understanding *bara*—as conveying functions, or "moral intentions"—is illustrated in Psalm 119. "Your word, Lord, is eternal; it stands firm in the heavens. Your faithfulness continues through all generations; you established the earth, and it endures. Your laws endure to this day, for all things serve you. If your law had not been my delight, I would have perished in my affliction. I will never forget your precepts, for by them you have preserved my life" (vv. 89–93; see Ps. 1).

34. See Jenson, *Systematic Theology, Volume 2*, 8, n. 35. Christopher B. Kaiser offers several helpful summaries of the way God's relationship to the world as Creator was understood in *Creational Theology and the History of Physical Science: The Creationist Tradition from Basil to Bohr*, Studies in the History of Christian Thought, Vol. 78 (New York: Brill, 1997), 132, 175.

the world is not something humans, or any creature, can rise to (not even to be co-creator), and any attempt to decree our own norms into the world's functioning is improperly playacting at being divine (which is sin).[29]

This ancient sense of "creating" (*bara*) would mean we would have to wait until Genesis 1:2–2:3 to hear God opening up creation's life through *creating* the heavens and earth; we have to get to the seven days for any creative activity. One way of reading verse 1 has been to make it a report about a creative (productive) action that occurs prior to the seven days—in other words, reading verse 1 to mean that, at a beginning point, God produced a raw heavens and earth. In this approach, verse 2 is interpreted as a description of what God produced in verse 1. Then, over seven days, Genesis 1 says what God did with that initial creation. This interpretation is called "double-creation."[30] Generally this approach has been taken by Christians who are trying to harmonize this passage with a belief in creation out of nothing. However, the idea of creation out of nothing did not arise until the second century of Christianity.[31] The

---

119 (see vv. 137–144). There is a difference between creaturely disobedience (which leads to death) and God's dominion being threatened.

29. As Jenson suggests: "The notion that creatures should or could be 'co-creators' is, if 'create' is intended to mean what it does in Scripture, simply oxymoronic" (*Systematic Theology, Volume 2*, 5, n. 17).

30. William P. Brown, *Structure, Role, and Ideology in the Hebrew and Greek Texts of Genesis 1:1–2:3*, SBLDS 132 (Atlanta: Scholars Press, 1993), 35. Coleson takes an approach to verses 1–2 that could be interpreted in the direction of double creation (*Genesis 1–11*, 39–45; see also Copan and Craig, *Creation Out of Nothing*, 60–65).

31. Scholars continue to look for, but not find, evidence for a doctrine of creation out of nothing that is older than Theophilus of Antioch in the second century AD. As Brown states, "no concrete instance can be cited that proves that the doctrine existed by the time the [Septuagint] was written. In fact, more evidence to the contrary can be marshaled" (Brown, *Structure, Role, and Ideology*, 34f.). The Septuagint is a translation of the OT into Greek that was done in the final centuries BCE. The Septuagint is the oldest-surviving manuscript of the OT that we have. The ancient Near Eastern cultures and Greek-influenced cultures of the Mediterranean started their creation narratives with a preexisting condi-

In the Old Testament, God is not just a one-time Creator of the world and its inhabitants in the beginning; our Redeemer-Creator-Ruler creates *throughout* the biblical narrative.[35] A key example is that God *created* Israel by first calling Abraham and Sarah out of their Mesopotamian roots *for* the purpose of blessing the nations (Gen. 12:1–3). Later, God *created* Israel by separating their enslaved descendants from Egypt and communicating to them the terms of a covenant—that is, what was to be the character and arrangement of their life. In their intended function in the world, this people were to walk according to the paths of the Torah, according to God's will for them. Because of God's creative action, a people come to exist that did not exist before (Isa. 43:1, 7, 15)—even if Abraham and Sarah, or the enslaved Hebrews, were alive before being newly established by God. What comes to exist in Genesis is a world that is alive and bountifully filled, not a hopeless, empty waste. What comes to exist with Abraham and Sarah is a bountiful people to bless the nations (Gen. 12:1–3), not a childless, futureless couple (11:30). What comes to exist with their enslaved descendants is a priestly nation, not an enslaved people (Exod. 19:1–6).

How Does Genesis 1 Look in Comparison?

The idea of creation being primarily about *making a new situation that is to function according to divine purposes* is not unique to Israel in the ancient world. We can see this notion of creating at work among other ancient Near Eastern cultures. In one Egyptian teaching, Ra's creative word carried with it the principle of *ma'at* (order, justice, and harmony—function) and *heka* (magic—power for life).[36]

---

35. See Coleson, *Genesis 1–11*, 45.
36. Joshua J. Mark, "Ma'at," *Ancient History Encyclopedia*, https://www.ancient.eu/Ma%27at/.

The key thing to note is where Israel's texts are *different* from the general thinking of their time.

Ra's command conveys organizing principle and life-power. Ra's word is effective in accomplishing what it intends. Even so, that does not mean various cultures understood the character and creative intentions of their gods the same way. Ra did not intend for the world (or Egypt) to function according to the same order, justice, and harmony as Genesis 1 teaches about God. We can see that biblical teaching shows starkly different views from other ancient texts about God's creative governance. For example, in Psalm 119, God's decrees have the character of love, righteousness, and wisdom. They result in salvation, life, and delight for those who follow in God's way.

Babylon's Enuma Elish is a clear example of stark difference to Genesis 1. At the start of Enuma Elish, many gods are birthed within the primal waters of Apsu and Tiamat. Yet *creation*, in the proper sense, did not take place for a while because "no destinies had been decreed."[37] The gods did not have places or functions yet. In fact, that was precisely the problem. They continuously jumbled around within their water-parents, having no places, functions, or sense of time—like when it was sleeping time or partying time. Because their water-father, Apsu, became threateningly enraged over the constant disturbances, they killed him; then they elected Marduk to go into battle against their water-mother, Tiamat, and her army general. A key detail is that Tiamat bestowed on her general the Tablet of Destinies before the battle with Marduk. Thus, her general "decreed destinies for the gods" who served under him.[38] When Marduk killed Tiamat and subdued her general, Marduk took the Tablet

---

37. Enuma Elish, Tablet I:8, https://www.ancient.eu/article/225/enuma-elish—-the-babylonian-epic-of-creation—-fu/. As Westermann says, "The beginning is not an act of creation but a succession of births. Creation is but a consequence of the drama which is beginning" (28).

38. Enuma Elish, Tablet II:46.

of Destinies for himself.[39] Marduk already had agreement from the other gods that, if he won, it would be his utterance that would decree destinies.[40] With the Tablet now in hand, Marduk *created* the world by mercilessly dismembering Tiamat: smashing her skull, severing her arteries, and dividing her body in half.[41] Out of her he formed all the parts of the heavens and earth, setting patterns to the world and places for all the gods.[42] The *mercy* Marduk shows in the text is for the gods—not for the world or earth's creatures. In fact, humans were made from the blood of Tiamat's condemned general, so that all the gods would be free from ever having to work again. Since Tiamat's general prompted Tiamat to fight against the assembly of the gods, humans would forever serve the gods' needs.[43]

The brutality of Marduk the warrior is terrifying. He wields winds to imprison and torment, a club to smash, and a bow to kill.[44] Even the very substance of the creation he ordered is a constant reminder that Marduk should not—indeed, cannot—be challenged. He decorates using his enemies' corpses. Within the heavens and earth (this cosmic monument to Marduk's conquest), human existence and toil are an endless sentence of slavery for daring to battle the gods. This is according to Marduk's declaration of destinies.

Genesis 1 could not be more different in its portrayal of God as Creator and God's economy for the heavens and earth.[45] For starters, there is no enmity between God and

---

39. Enuma Elish, Tablet IV:121.
40. Enuma Elish, Tablet II:160.
41. Enuma Elish, Tablet IV:121–37.
42. Enuma Elish, Tablet IV:138–V:72.
43. Enuma Elish, Tablet VI:1–36.
44. Enuma Elish, Tablet IV:27–101.
45. George Smith first published his translation of Enuma Elish in 1876 under the title "The Chaldean Account of Genesis." The title alone suggested that Genesis and Enuma Elish were directly connected, Genesis being based on the

the waters (*mayim*) of the primal deep (*tehom*, v. 2). There is no struggle, no conquest, and no dismemberment.[46] The deep (*tehom*) is not even a divine-like character with whom God could contend in such a way.[47] Early Christians understood the text this way. Basil the Great wrote, "'The deep' is not a fullness of antithetical powers, as some fantasize, nor is the darkness an original and evil force arrayed against the good."[48] Instead, verse 2 describes this dark, watery condition of "the earth" (*'eres*) as a wasteland—"desolate and empty" (*tohu wabohu*).[49] It is an uncultivated (untouched), unproductive (non-functioning) earth—which parallels the recurring issues of barrenness and famine in the rest of Genesis.

Many English versions translate *tohu* in verse 2 as "formless" and *bohu* as "void."[50] The scholarship on the

---

older Enuma Elish. The early trend in comparative scholarship—of emphasizing similarities, agreement, or dependence between texts—has transitioned into attention to different meanings the texts convey through nuanced differences in their details. For cautions against some of the mistakes in methodology since the 1800s, see Vail, *Creation and Chaos Talk*, 11–12, 15, 95–97 (notes 97 and 98).

46. See Westermann, *Genesis 1–11*, 27–34, especially 31.

47. Connections between terms from different ancient languages and ideas in their creation accounts have been deconstructed in several ways. See David T. Tsumura, *Creation and Destruction: A Reappraisal of the Chaoskampf Theory in the Old Testament* (Winona Lake, IN: Eisenbrauns, 2005), 36–42; B. Alister, "Tiamat," *Dictionary of Deities and Demons in the Bible*, 1634–1639, ed. Karel van der Toorn, Bob Becking, and Pieter W. van der Horst (New York: Brill, 1995), 1638; Rebecca Watson, *Chaos Uncreated: A Reassessment of the Theme of "Chaos" in the Hebrew Bible* (Berlin: de Gruyter, 2005), 24; and Coleson, *Genesis 1–11*, 42–43.

48. Basil the Great, *Hexaemeron*, ii.4; quoted in Jenson, *Systematic Theology, Volume 2*, 11.

49. Tsumura, *Creation and Destruction*, 75. In verse 2, "the deep" is included within the reference to "the earth;" the deep is part of the earth. The earth/deep is "not yet productive and inhabitable and without light" (68–69; Tsumura walks through the use of *tohu* in the other nineteen OT occurrences and how they help us understand Genesis 1:2; see *Creation and Destruction*, 21–35). In short, *tohu* refers to a desert wilderness or waste (see Westermann, *Genesis 1–11*, 103). Terence Fretheim also concludes that this descriptor means the earth is "desolate and unproductive" (Fretheim, "The Book of Genesis," *NIB*, 342).

50. See a sample of comparisons: https://www.biblestudytools.com/genesis/1-2-compare.html.

Hebrew terms has been moving away from these abstract ideas toward a concrete description for a type of desolate, empty land. *Tohu* and *bohu* is a condition like what Israel's land became after Babylon destroyed their homes and took them into captivity. Abstract words like "formless" and "void" are influenced by a long history of interpreting Genesis 1 in conversation with the Greek philosophical idea of creation from formless matter.[51] Greek thinking emphasizes material and form—what something is made *out of* and what *shape* it has.[52] The Greek idea of a primordial formless matter (*khora*) entered the conversation after Genesis 1 was written, in an environment where Israel's theology interacted with Greek thinking.[53] Even while the use of certain Greek ideas was challenged by some Christian authors,[54] "at least since Philo of Alexandria (20 BCE–50 CE) early Jewish and Christian interpreters of Genesis 1 have noted, if not exploited, certain similarities between Plato's *Timaeus* and the priestly account of creation."[55]

---

51. Westermann, *Genesis 1–11*, 109.

52. In Christianity's history, this trend came out of interacting with Plato's *Timaeus*. Platonism eventually systematized the idea of world formation into three principles: God, Ideas (form), and Matter. We westerners now think about creation in terms of *matter* (out of what did God create?) and *form* (what structure did God create?). See May, *Creatio Ex Nihilo*, 2–4.

53. Westermann, *Genesis 1–11*, 109–10.

54. Rebecca Watson points to objections from Hippolytus, "Refutation of All Heresies," and Methodius, "Extracts from the Work on Things Created" (*Chaos Uncreated*, 13).

55. William P. Brown, "Divine Act and the Art of Persuasion in Genesis 1," *History and Interpretation: Essays in Honour of John H. Hayes*, ed. M. Patrick Graham, William P. Brown, and Jeffrey K. Kuan, Journal for the Study of the Old Testament Supplement Series 173 (Sheffield, UK: Sheffield Academic Press, 1993), 19. Harmonizing Genesis 1:2 with the *khora* (eternally existing formless matter) of Plato's *Timaeus* continued through the Middle Ages (Willemien Otten, "Reading Creation: Early Medieval Views of Genesis and Plato's *Timaeus*," *The Creation of Heaven and Earth: Re-Interpretations of Genesis 1 in the Context of Judaism, Ancient Philosophy, Christianity, and Modern Physics*, ed. George H. van Kooten [Boston: Brill, 2005], 240–41).

However, as we have seen, the emphasis with *bara* is on divine intent—*torah* for the world's operation. The emphasis of the Genesis narrative is not so much a movement from formless to formed, or disordered to ordered. It is from not yet divinely intended to divinely intended, or from purposeless and functionless to purposeful and functional. In other words, God has yet to communicate. The situation moves from not yet expressed to expressed. To be without or apart from divine intent is an empty wasteland; to be within or following divine intent is flourishing life.[56]

"Formless" is a translation older than Christianity. A newer trend toward describing the conditions in Genesis 1:2 as "chaos" became popular after 1876. Chaos suggests something more ominous or sinister than even formless. However, this too has been deconstructed through careful examination.[57] In being true to Genesis 1, it is best to go in the direction of what the Hebrew terms meant—especially what they meant around the time of Israel's exile, when

---

56. As Susannah Ticciati says it, verse 2 is a context of indeterminacy into which God introduces distinctions in vv. 3–27. The various things that are distinguished from one another are not in opposition to one another. Even the distinctions God introduces are not in opposition to the indeterminacy of verse 2; instead, they "stand positively to it in a relation of actuality to potency" (Ticciati, "Anachronism or Illumination? Genesis 1 and Creation ex nihilo," *Anglican Theological Review* 99.4 [2017]: 707). Ticciati is not in favor of opposing order to disorder. The world is always unfolding. The potential for expression (indeterminacy) is not bad, only certain ways creation expresses itself. Other expressions out of that potency are good (see 708–709).

57. One area of my dissertation was to look into the history and appropriateness of using "chaos" to describe Genesis 1:2. The last 150 years have been the Wild West in how the term has been thrown around, and most every way it is used mischaracterizes Genesis 1. The word "chaos" has become a catchall for any idea people want to add into it from any culture, time period, or area of study. Not only does it mischaracterize Genesis 1, but it also implies questionable theology: a conflict at the deepest root of the relationship between creation and God. See Vail, *Creation and Chaos Talk: Charting a Way Forward*, Princeton Theological Monograph Series 185 (Eugene, OR: Pickwick Publications, 2012). Other scholars also hesitate to use the term "chaos." See Clifford, "*Creatio ex nihilo*," 57; Watson, *Chaos Uncreated*; Tsumura, *Creation and Destruction*.

many scholars suppose Genesis 1 was written. The tangible idea of empty wasteland is reinforced by looking at the appearance of *tohu* and *bohu* in prophetic texts (see, for example, Isa. 27:7–11; 32:9–15 and Jer. 4:23–28; 22:5–7). In these texts, God will remove disobedient Israel from their cities and lands. Having been emptied, the place will return to an uncultivated wasteland.[58] Israel saw this warning fulfilled when Babylon invaded and carried them into captivity. In the later chapters of Isaiah and in Genesis 1, Israel reflected on God's creative, redeeming work in the face of the empty wasteland they experienced.

Genesis 1:2 illustrates that the earth (inclusive of *the deep*) requires divine action if it is ever to be anything other than an unproductive, empty space. It has no God-given function. Without being *created*, it is not anything. It certainly has no inherent capacities. It must have divine intervention. Graciously, the divine wind of God—the Spirit of God—*hovers* over the face of the deep.[59] This fluttering over the water is a "positive intervention of God."[60] It evokes the idea of a mother bird over her young. It is not for God's benefit, like neutralizing a threat. Rather, the Spirit of God "is the pensive, creative, nurturing, soon-to-be-acting presence of God."[61] The Spirit is the only possibility of a way forward for the lifeless earth.

---

58. See Vail, *Atonement and Salvation: The Extravagance of God's Love* (Kansas City, MO: Beacon Hill Press of Kansas City, 2016), 23; 144, n. 5.

59. It is worth noting the movement of God's Spirit over this barren wasteland in connection with the promises given to Israel in Ezekiel 36 and the Spirit of God moving over the dry bones of Israel in Ezekiel 37. Some interpreters have interpreted *ruach Elohim* (wind/breath/spirit of God) in verse 2 as a "mighty wind" or "wind of divine magnitude," making the verse sound more like Marduk's terrorizing winds. However, "no other OT reference can warrant this translation" since God's *ruach* (wind/breath/spirit) "normally has a positive meaning" (Brevard S. Childs, *Myth and Reality in the Old Testament*, Studies in Biblical Theology, 2nd ed. [London: SCM Press Ltd., 1962], 36, 35).

60. Westermann, *Genesis 1–11*, 107.

61. Coleson, *Genesis 1–11*, 43.

The rest of Genesis supports these positive characterizations of God's engagement with the earth. God is mindful of people's circumstances (barren, near death, unloved, enslaved, unjustly treated, etc.) and addresses their troubles; God inquires, investigates, remembers, sees, hears, and is moved. So often God grants people in perilous or dead-end situations a way forward. Indeed, the first time anyone names God in the text is when Hagar, at the point of her rescue, exclaims, "You are the God who sees me" (16:13). God is the one who blesses and the one in whose name blessings are given.

In this most primal picture the author could paint, the Spirit of God was already present and active. There is no "not yet" circumstance where the Spirit of God is not already engaged, as the precondition for any story to unfold. The Spirit's work is the divine action that is named first; the Spirit's hovering presence anticipates a life story about to unfold.

So Then, Does God Create *out of* Something?

This may be the trickiest of the questions. Genesis 1 starts as an ancient Near Eastern narrative would, with a primal condition of waters and darkness. This is "the earth" in its empty wasteland condition (i.e., pre-creation). God's Spirit is hovering over what is described. It seems to be *something* and not *nothing*.[62] In the strictest sense, "the introductions to the creation stories known to us never make the step from 'when this and that was not yet' to 'when there was nothing.'"[63]

---

62. It is beyond the scope of this book to interact with Catherine Keller's reading of Genesis 1. She is adamant that we not turn the *tehom* of Genesis 1:2 into a nothing (no-thing). However, that is for other reasons related to her theological positions. For a challenging read, see Catherine Keller, *Face of the Deep: A Theology of Becoming* (New York: Routledge, 2003). I summarize and analyze her position in chapter 5 of *Creation and Chaos Talk*. Ticciati offers a helpful critique of Keller in "Anachronism or Illumination?", 691–712.

63. Westermann, *Genesis 1–11*, 44.

It is not enough, however, to leave our question here. The narrative is moving from "not yet," or "before" into the world we now inhabit.[64] While it is instructive that the text uses *tohu* ("wasteland") and *bohu* ("empty") as the contrasting image to the creative purposes God will introduce, the goal of the narrative "is not to describe a state that preceded creation but to mark off God's act of creation from a 'before' which is beyond words and can only be described in negative terms."[65] This aim can be further seen in the Septuagint translation of verse 2 from Hebrew into Greek.[66] It translated the Hebrew *tohu wabohu* into the Greek *aoratos kai akataskeuastos* ("invisible and not fully furnished or supplied," or "invisible and incompletely or inadequately furnished or supplied"). In Classical Greek, *akataskeuastos* was used to describe a ship, army, or caravan that did not have its necessary gear for a journey.[67] It is almost as though the Septuagint translators tried to capture all of *tohu wabohu* ("uncultivated and empty") with this second Greek word

---

64. Westermann, *Genesis 1–11*, 43–44.

65. Westermann, *Genesis 1–11*, 46.

66. We assume the Septuagint is a faithful guide in how to communicate the Hebrew Bible via the Greek language. While Bible scholars used to be suspicious of the Septuagint as a possible contamination of the Hebrew Bible, there has been a growing trend in the last few decades of appreciating the consistency in the Septuagint in picking a Greek term to use for each theological term in Hebrew. The Septuagint set a precedent of how to use the Greek language to communicate the faith of Israel as it had been worked out in its sacred texts. By claiming and reshaping a variety of Greek words to communicate certain concepts from the Hebrew Bible, New Testament authors benefited from that tradition of specialized Greek vocabulary and how to talk about God's work in Christ in the syntax of the Greek language. New Testament authors frequently quoted from the Septuagint when they wanted to quote the Hebrew Bible. The Septuagint was the guide and trusted source for the early church in explaining the Christian faith across the Roman Empire. See, for example, R. Timothy McLay, *The Use of the Septuagint in New Testament Research* (Grand Rapids: Eerdmans, 2003). Regarding the Septuagint and Genesis 1, see Brown, *Structure, Role, and Ideology*.

67. Thanks to Kevin Hawthorne for his translation of *akataskeuastos* and explanation of how it was used in Classical Greek.

(*akataskeuastos*: "not provisioned"). The first Greek word (*aoratos*: "invisible") is not in the Hebrew text. It seems to offer a cultural explanation about ancient Near Eastern creation narratives in the direction that modern commentators go. That is, we are not to imagine that Genesis 1:2 describes a time, place, or material that God created "out of." Rather, it is "invisible" (see Heb. 11:3). Since creating had not begun (all the work of speaking, making, separating, setting, evaluating, and blessing), verse 2 starts with "(functional) nonexistence."[68] There is the presence of the Spirit. However, nothing that will be the heavens and earth is yet *created* by God. No situation of purposeful function has been given to anything at all. Everything in the heavens and the earth is *created* because of and under God's governance. Before verse 3, nothing exists as part of the heavens and the earth because God had not created its existence within the heavens and the earth.

Verse 2 fits the ancient method for narrating a beginning. These types of sentences made "it possible for the old creation narratives to describe creation as an event or as an act. Acts and events occur only in a series in any given narrative, linked in some way to what has gone before."[69] The method of communication—narrative—requires we start *somewhere* so an action can be said to take place *there*, even if the first action is thought to mark *the beginning*. We should be cautious of making too much of the *something* described in verse 2 (like the waters and darkness), even while it is jumping ahead in the history of ideas to say that the author was claiming there was *nothing* before God created. Such an idea did not exist yet. Even if it did, "one can teach *creatio ex nihilo*; but one cannot narrate it."[70] Even to

---

68. See Coleson's description of John Walton's position (*Genesis 1–11*, 41).
69. Westermann, *Genesis 1–11*, 46.
70. Westermann, *Genesis 1–11*, 46.

narrate "before God created there was nothing—no time, substance, or space" is to turn the *nothing* into *something* that *was not*. If we try to imagine *nothing*, our mind has *something* in it. Narrating or imagining *nothing* turns *nothing* into the *context* in which the first action is narrated. In this case, creation comes out of the *something* (the space, vacuum, darkness) we imagined. Narrating creation out of *nothing* necessitates saying *something*. To tell the story that God created the heavens and the earth (everything) requires something like verse 2. In sum, Israel's method of narrative required they start somewhere. The description provided in verse 2 offers rich insights into what the passage has to say about the cosmos and God's relationship with it. Even so, we can make too much of the primal condition, as if to wrongly imagine it is the primordial material out of which God makes the heavens and the earth.

Genesis 1 actually differs from its two major neighbors on what to make of the waters. On one side, Egyptian belief moves from primordial water to a creation. Egypt's primordial water, Nun, "was the 'milieu within which creation unfolds.'"[71] Even more, Nun is more than a passive space or substance. It was "a 'mythic symbol of the abstract reality of the full potential of being.'"[72] In other words, what differs from Egypt to Israel is that for Egypt there is potency in Nun. Their god Ptah took this potency for himself in order to create himself and then everything else. For Israel, potency is not in the empty wasteland. The waters of Genesis 1 are not a pregnant, generative potency out of which the world springs. Potency is of God and God's initiative. Verse 2 is an empty wasteland upon which the Spirit of God hovers.

On Israel's other side, Babylon's Enuma Elish says Marduk formed the heavenly dome, the land, mountains,

---

71. Brown quoting Allen, *Structure, Role, and Ideology*, 180f.
72. Brown quoting V. A. Tobin, *Structure, Role, and Ideology*, 180.

and rivers *out of* Tiamat's slain body. It is a critical distinction that Genesis 1 does not make the waters and darkness of verse 2 into the building blocks for all of creation—the materials God used. To be absolutely precise about it, "the Bible is silent about the material from which the universe was formed."[73] In Genesis 1, the heavens and earth are not made out of what already existed. That is a significant affirmation of Christianity's teaching about creation out of nothing.

Greek culture is what made substance and form such a big deal in the way Westerners frame their experience of the world and what they want a creation story to explain. Westerners want to know where the material comes from and have long clarified that it comes *out of nothing*. Genesis 1 is simply not answering questions Western culture prejudices us to ask. It does not say what things are made out of, nor does it go the other direction and say they are made out of nothing. Genesis 1 is focused on *making a new* (previously nonexistent) *situation that is to function according to divine purposes*. Thus, there is not an explicit *out of* doctrine in this text since it is not operating within or pushing an explicit *out of* perspective. It may be maddening to us to be left asking what we are to make of the waters and darkness. Perhaps the most fitting answer is the direction Christianity has gone: we make *nothing* of it!

God exists without coming into being or being created. God has the authority and capacity to rule-create without having to seize it, be given it, or grow into it. Even so, there is no kingdom to rule—or anything that is being ruled; rather, the before-creation situation is untilled and unfilled. There is only the Spirit's anticipatory presence. A heaven and earth must be created. A domain must be made that is to function according to the Ruler's purposes. No kingdom functionally exists. While God has no beginning,

---

73. Watson, *Chaos Uncreated*, 18, n. 30.

the whole of created reality does have a beginning—the heavens and the earth. While God has the capacity to function as Ruler-Creator-Redeemer and the Spirit of God is active as the possibility of there being a kingdom of subjects over which to rule, it is not until day 1 that any divine purposes mark the start of God ruling-creating, and having a domain with subjects. Day 1 marks the beginning of anything coming to exist (function) as a subject of the Ruler-Creator. There is nothing of creation before day 1—only God, the Uncreated One.

Initial Conclusions

The first two verses of Genesis 1 already say a great deal within their ancient context.

First, this creation account names God (*Elohim*) as the actor—although *Elohim* is not technically God's name (see Exod. 3). Saying God (*Elohim*) is Creator already challenges any narrative claiming a different god orchestrated creation.

Second, the heavens and the earth have a beginning, but nowhere does it say God has a beginning. God *is*, period. God does not emerge from the primal waters, as though the waters birth God or God self-forms out of the waters. Other people's gods came from another substance or another god.

Third, no material or agency outside of God causes God's existence, which would make God beholden to or dependent on something else. God is in no way secondary to anything above God or more primal than God.

Fourth, God is distinct in being and substance from the heavens and the earth. Other gods were often associated with a worldly realm. God is not associated with either a substance or realm of the heavens or earth but is distinct from the heavens and earth. We know nothing of God's "substance," and we do not worship something in the world as God or God's substance.[74]

Fifth, God is not one among many divine beings. There is one God.

Sixth, God does not have to ascend into God's position, prove God's capabilities to a council, or gain the authority to create.

Seventh, we do not hear of any need in God for why God had to create—such as God was getting old, had no place to stand, wanted someone else to do work, or was in danger from the waters. God was not under pressure or being begged by a pantheon. Creation was also not some type of naturalistic outflow of a male-female intermingling. By not naming any external pressure or natural generation, Genesis 1 suggests that creation is God's free, gracious choice.

Eighth, the primal waters do not have their own divine-like powers of production. The situation is unproductive and empty without God's action. Creation is not an outflow of natural forces or properties of matter. Creation takes a Creator, and that Creator provides all things necessary for creation, in order that creation itself may operate in the economy of God's *torah*.

---

74. In a more technical sense, we do not know God in God's essence but in God's relating to us (revelation).

FOUR

Genesis 1
Dwelling

In the last two chapters we have been getting our bearings, locating ourselves against the backdrop of ancient Near Eastern ways of thinking about the world and where Israel fit in relation to those views. We have also been looking at the place of Genesis 1 in the Bible and a host of considerations in its self-introduction (vv. 1–2). Having entered into the text, in this chapter we are going to dwell in the space of Genesis 1 (meaning 1:1–2:3). My hope is that, in our mind's eye, the text will become immediately present to us, less located a long distance in time from where we are now, ages ago at the dawn of all things. We will see ourselves, right now, as participants in the same world God awakens in the text; we will faithfully live out our function in God's good creation, according to the purposes of our Ruler-Creator-Redeemer. In other words, this text will surround us as *torah* for our present life with God and all creation. If our Creator is blessing the world with life-affirming pathways, we ought to hear and heed them. Even more, this text does not stop at day six with humans dwelling in the world. It goes on to day seven with God being at home in the world. The heavens and the earth are a shared dwelling. May our eyes be opened to the world around us and the mutuality shared among all its participants.

Days 1–3

The Spirit of God hovers where there is no story yet (v. 2). The Spirit's brooding anticipates a coming story, like the coming birth of a child. Indeed, the Spirit's activity over an impossible situation even makes possible that a creation (something other than God) will now have an unfolding story with the God who always was, is, and will be. With the already present Spirit, a word (Word) from God calls out, "Let there be . . ." This Word evokes. While it voices divine intention, it anticipates obedient response. Any instruction or command awaits reply. The story of this world starts and proceeds with divine initiative, direction, and empowerment. Yet God will not be the lone actor in this creation. The Spirit anticipates—indeed, makes possible—a response to the evoking Word. Through the Spirit and Word, God opens space for more than just God in this story. God's creative work of calling, making, separating, setting, naming, evaluating, and blessing is not to be a solo performance. God's creative actions make possible creation's "own varied activity"—such as separating, ruling, bringing forth, and reproducing.[1] There is interplay with Creator and creation through the narrative. As a result, "the creature's own activity is constitutively bound up in the process of creation."[2] God opens up time and eternity to be more than a story of God alone; God generously makes room for all creation—the heavens and the earth. Through

---

1. Michael Welker, "What is Creation? Rereading Genesis 1 and 2," *Theology Today* 48.1 (Apr 1991): 64.

2. Welker, "What is Creation?" 64. There are implications of God working for the sake of creation's participation. As Welker continues, "God creates by bringing different realms of life into fruitful associations of interdependent relations that promote life." Each of God's subjects is "fruitfully bringing itself into these associations of interdependent realms" (64). Every interconnected part acts for the benefit of the whole.

God's Spirit and Word, God blesses creation to share and express itself in the beauty of God's own life.

Early in the narrative there is not much that the uncultivated, empty earth is said to *do* in response to God's creative speaking. God said, "Let there be light," and there was light in the world (v. 3). God said, "Let there be a vault between the waters to separate water from water" (v. 6). God made this vault and did the work of separating the waters into water under and water above the vault (v. 7).[3] Having a vault over our heads is a foreign concept to contemporary readers. This idea of a firm object (a vault or dome) above the earth that held up the waters and all the heavenly bodies (sun, moon, stars) was common in ancient thinking. Israel's writings indicate that God provided regular rains from that heavenly storehouse (Deut. 28:12) and completely opened the windows in the vault at the time of the flood (see Gen. 7:11 in the NRSV).

On the third day, God told the water below to gather in order to "let dry ground appear" (v. 9; see Ps. 104:5–9). The waters are not addressed until verse 9. They have not yet been called to a purpose. As far as the unfolding world is concerned, they are functionally nonexistent. With God's creative action of verse 9, the waters below are now to function as "seas" and the dry ground as "land." To function as seas is to be gathered apart from the dry ground. To be land is to be tasked with producing vegetation (v. 11).

Each of the first three days define *spaces*, or *domains* in the world: alternating *light* and *dark* give the domains of day and night; contrasting *above* and *below* give the domains of heavens and earth; distinguishing *water* from *dry ground* creates the domains of sea and land. In these three days,

---

3. Note that God accomplishes everything in the narrative associated with the heavens—"and there was light" (v. 3), "God made the vault and separated" the waters (v. 7), and "God made two great lights" and "also made the stars" (v. 16).

time and space—as we might think of them—are called forth. Sequence is introduced with alternations from light to dark to light—evening and morning. All space—in their limited understanding of the universe's size—is defined (top to bottom and side to side).

We might be tempted in these first days to figure out how photons of light could be separated from darkness (which is the absence of photons), or if Hebrew people thought of darkness as a substance (that could be "over the surface of the deep" or "separated" from light). We might also, for that matter, be tempted to figure out how the primal waters were not solid ice when there was no light to heat them.[4] In their worldview, the point of focus in a creation narrative was divine purpose. Light and dark are *for* respective domains, or periods of day and night (v. 5).[5] The "darkness" of verse 2 was functionally nonexistent in relation to God's creation of the heavens and the earth, having no place or function. It simply served as the start of the narrative, giving us the not-yet-created earth. Then, in a divine act of *creation*, darkness was given a place and function in the heavens and earth, to serve, opposite of light, as night (v. 5). The realm above—so far consisting of a dome and water—was to serve as "the heavens" (same Hebrew word in v. 8 as in v. 1). And, like darkness, the verse 2 waters of the not-yet-created earth—with no place or function in God's creation—were *now created* in the heavens and earth to serve as seas so that dry ground could serve as vegetation-producing land.

Days 1–3 are about all domains of life—everywhere, at any time, is covered. Genesis 1 does not challenge the

---

4. I wish I could remember which of my students first raised this point in class. Even though you remain anonymous, I thank you. It was a great observation. Please accept my apology for my memory lapse.

5. Walton's interpretation of verses 3-5 is worth reading (*The Lost World of Genesis One*, 54–56). Though I do not follow him all the way to his conclusion, he has influenced my reading of these verses.

structure of how ancient Near Eastern people thought the cosmos was shaped when it narrates that God created them. Many things do not work for modern science: to have a flat earth with a dome and water over it, a planet forming without first having a star, or alternating periods of day and night without the sun. This does not mean, however, that Genesis 1 is irrelevant. We have already seen the manner in which God engages creation, and that God has intentions for all domains without exception. The presence and activities of the Spirit and Word are the very provision for all domains of space and time—for all that exists from heaven to earth. God cultivates a space of mutuality, which can and will unfold in a bountiful narrative of divine-creaturely fellowship. Whether we are ancient or modern, we can appreciate that we share in this sacred cosmic space with God and all else. The rest of the narrative will offer us further instruction on God's intentions.

Days 4–6

The narrative sequence of Genesis 1 moves through seven days. That straight line of one day after another can hide the repetition in pattern between days 1–3 and days 4–6. Each set of three days is like two parallel foundations. Each *space* God created in days 1–3 (with its intended functions) is revisited, in order, in days 4–6. In the second set, the various domains are alive in their functions as they support their respective inhabitants. Here is what that looks like:

DOMAINS	INHABITANTS
Day 1 Light and separation from darkness	**Day 4** Lights of day and night
Day 2 Dome and waters above (heavens) and waters below (earth)	**Day 5** Birds in the dome (heavens/sky) and creatures in the waters below
Day 3 Separation of gathered waters (seas) and dry, plant-producing ground (land)	**Day 6** Animals and humans to fill the land

Many of us modern Westerners operate, whether consciously or otherwise, on the assumption that the universe is more like a machine, clicking along by cause-and-effect processes, according to laws of nature. The world to us is simply a lifeless stage upon which living things act out their stories. We divide our thinking between organic and inorganic, animate and inanimate. This is not the imagination the authors of the Scriptures carried. To them, every creation of God is blessed by God to function as a faithful subject under its Creator, the Ruler (Ps. 145:9–13). The heavens can rejoice, the earth can be glad, mountains can sing, seas can praise, fields and forests can be jubilant, and wilderness places can be glad and rejoice (see 1 Chron. 16:31; Pss. 69:34; 96:11–12; Isa. 35:1; 49:13). Our environment is not simply background. Even more, nothing in all creation is merely raw material or resource *for* human use, according to human purposes. Everything is blessed by our common Ruler *for* a purpose given by the Creator-Ruler; everything is called to serve in its intended role *for* the thriving of the whole community, in and to the glory of its loving Creator.

There is God-ordained *torah* in effect among each created thing that humankind should not overwrite or rewrite. We do so only to the destruction of ourselves and all fellow creation. The only law we can write is a law of sin and death (e.g., Rom. 5:12; 8:2).

It is important to clarify further what it means for things in the world to be *for* a purpose. Filtered through a modern Western lens, it might be tempting for Christians to think that all things in creation exist *for* humans to use in a certain way. We might hear it as though everything is a resource, or tool, that humans are supposed to use according to its purpose or function *for us*. This thinking flows in the wrong direction; it flows in a top-down direction of what humans do to or with God's creation. Thus, it imagines we are lone, sovereign actors within a lifeless landscape, filled with brute animals. Humans are the top of the pyramid, with everything below us existing *for us*—so long as we use it correctly. This is not the teaching of Genesis 1.

Instead, God calls each part of creation to action; each part has a contribution to make in response to God's self-giving for it, through Spirit and Word. Humans are not to seize, use, or manipulate the world as though each feature is to function *for us*—for our own self-serving reasons. In Genesis 1, the flow of God and everything in God's world is *for* the good of others. Each part of God's creation is to respond to God's self-giving in a way that itself is self-giving for the well-being of creation's life. Each part is not to be owned and used. Each part has its own integrity from God to function according to its God-given *vocation* (from the Latin *vocare*, "to call"). It acts in giving itself. Its giving of itself is to be received and enjoyed by others as a gift for the flourishing of creation. It should be received as an act of love—not as something to be owned or used. All creation is called to live in mutual fellowship. As we will see on day 6, humans too have a God-given function to give of themselves for the flourishing of life in creation. We are not here *for* domination; we are chief-servant, according to the character of God's own self-giving. Creation's Redeemer-Creator-Ruler operates chiefly in self-giving, other-nurturing love.

Day 4

Light and dark mark the periods of day and night. On day 4—the corresponding day to day 1—God placed lights in the dome of the heavens (Gen. 1:14–18). These lights (inhabitants) were not only to function with light and dark in distinguishing day and night (vv. 14, 18), but their function was also to communicate for all creation additional times that organize what we do: "let them serve as signs to mark sacred times, and days and years" (v. 14). The lights are *for* telling us all what the present *time* is for. Not every minute, hour, day, week, month, or year is the same as every other—in other words, one endless blur of sameness. Different times are intended *for* different activities. When evening comes, the present day is over.[6] Darkness dictates that it is the time for rest—to begin the new day by entrusting ourselves, through taking refreshment, into the care of the One from whom all blessings flow. Morning brings with it the light of day, the time for wakefulness and stepping actively into what God has provided and makes possible.

Furthermore, in night and day, God has graciously given lights to illuminate the goings-on of the earth (v. 15). The lights not only mark off individual days, but they also help us mark the time for resting on the Sabbath (Exod. 23:12), sacred festivals (Gen. 1:14–19), Sabbath years (Gen.

---

6. Unlike the present idea that a calendar day begins at midnight or that we start our day when we wake, in Hebrew thought, the next day began at sundown. Thus, for example, Sabbath starts at sundown on Friday and ends at sundown on Saturday. It is puzzling that there would be evening and morning on day one (v. 5). Without a sun or light before day one, having evening (the shift from the prior day's light to this first day's dark) does not make sense.

1:10–11; Lev. 25:1–7), and the year of Jubilee (Lev. 25:8–55). The work of the lights is to be received as an overflowing gift. Observing these rest times is not primarily for our own personal benefit, but it is our service for the poor, the indebted, the enslaved, foreigners, future generations, domesticated and wild animals, and the land (Exod. 23:10–12; Lev. 25). God's creative intent overflows with grace; it is not that of a driving taskmaster. What it is *time for* us all to do is governed according to the rhythmic timekeeping of the lights.[7] And so much of that time is *for* gracious action toward the world around us.

We may find it odd that light is given its own day before and separate from light *sources*. It is especially odd that there are three *days* and a plant-producing land before there is a sun. We can pardon the author, however, when we see the symmetry in the six-day narrative structure that the separation of light and lights helped construct. Literary symmetry, for the sake of its theological implications, took priority here. Readers in the ancient Near East would have found this same part provocative for other reasons. In most every other culture, the moon and sun were created early and were among the highest-ranking gods. The Babylonians also considered the stars to be gods of various greatness, indicated by how brightly they shone. Some cultures tracked the movements of the heavenly bodies in order to read messages or omens from the gods' activities. Genesis 1 strips all of this away. The lights are not gods. The Hebrew words for "sun" and "moon" are not even used, so readers from various Semitic languages could not hear a word that might

---

7. In his novel *Jayber Crow*, Wendell Berry wonderfully illustrates how two people can practice farming in two different ways. One person wrongly uses land and time for himself, according to his purposes; the other respects what the land and time are *for*. The first person spreads a wake of carnage behind him; the second lives a peaceful, satisfied life. Berry, *Jayber Crow: A Novel* (Berkeley, CA: Crosspoint, 2000); see especially the chapter "Forsaking All Others," 176–87.

sound like the name of one of their gods. Instead, these features in the heavenly dome are not divine, and their only message is given from the lone God—that is, what the present time is for. The message does not change.

Day 5

Day 5 populates the spaces of day 2—the dome of the heavens and the waters below. We can see in the text the way God's gracious activities turn the uncultivated wasteland of verse 2 into productive response. God calls to the water: "Let the water teem with living creatures, and let birds fly above the earth across the vault of the sky" (v. 20). The waters are tasked with the created function of "swarming forth swarming living-things" (v. 20, author's translation). They are to support inhabitants.

It may be strange in a single command to connect the swarming of water creatures with the flying about of birds on the face of the heavenly dome over the earth. Putting water and air inhabitants together on the same day does not cohere with fossil records and current theories of evolutionary biology. However, it was common for ancient Near Eastern people to associate birds with water. Their observations of the way birds operated made the connection natural. For example: "The birds of the sky nest by the waters" (Ps. 104:12). Thus, creation narratives of the various cultures often brought the origin of water and air inhabitants together: "One can point to a widespread ancient Near Eastern tradition reaching as far back as the Sumerian and early Egyptian mythographers in which water plays a positive role in the formation of not only water creatures but also aerial creatures."[8]

---

8. Brown, *Structure, Role, and Ideology*, 184. It is noteworthy that, like what we see in Genesis 1:20, "water is often described in Egyptian cosmogonies as having a creative link not only with aquatic creatures such as fish, but also with birds" (181).

Again, we can appreciate the continued symmetry in the Genesis 1 narrative in the second set of three days, of populating what was established in the first set of three days. A preoccupation with whether ancient Near Eastern perceptions hold up to modern science should not detract from the theology of Genesis 1. God's life-breathing Spirit and evocative Word bring forth the world as the opposite of uncultivated, barren space. The environments themselves are not lifeless backgrounds, mere containers, for the story of living things; they are given roles *in* the story. They are given by our Creator to be *for* the swarming and darting-about of many kinds of living inhabitants. They have a *vocation*.

Current readers may also find something else puzzling about day 5. The water inhabitants include "great sea monsters" (*tannin*; v. 21, NRSV).[9] Timothy Beal suggests "that we can learn something about a religious tradition by getting to know its monsters, and that we learn something about monsters by looking into their religious backgrounds."[10] In short, "both monsters and religions are always culturally specific."[11] Monsters are so revealing because they usually represent what is opposed to the world as various religions frame it; monsters do not fit the system or make sense according to how they imagine things ought to work. Monsters are typically anomalies that *intrude into* and *threaten* their sense of the world—what feels homey to them.[12]

Israel's neighbors had legends about monster- or dragon-like creatures in the pre-creation era. These were

---

9. *Tannin* has several different uses in the OT. As Tyler R. Yoder notes, "Out of 14 total attestations in the [Hebrew Bible], *tannīn* carries explicit connotations of a 'common' snake in Exod. 7:9–10, 12; Deut. 32:33; and possibly Ps. 91:9, 13 while the other nine references imbue it with mythological overtones" (Yoder, "Ezekiel 29:3 and Its Ancient Near Eastern Context," *Vetus Testamentum* 63 [2013]: 488).

10. Timothy K. Beal, *Religion and Its Monsters* (New York: Routledge, 2002), 4.

11. Beal, *Religion and Its Monsters*, 8.

12. Beal, *Religion and Its Monsters*, 4.

primordial, uncreated forces or elements that came before, and did not belong to the categories of the divine creative intentions that would eventually govern the coming world. In the legends about this era before creation, great battles were fought by one of the gods against these powerful, primordial foes in order to subdue or kill them. These myths could give Israel's neighbors comfort that any unsettling agents that did not belong "in the house" had already been subjected under the power of their creator-god—or at least that their god was capable of protecting them when any monsters did intrude in their lives.[13]

Genesis 1 disrupts the norm for monsters in general and ancient Near Eastern monsters in particular. Genesis 1 has no primordial monsters—no hostile agents or forces. God is the lone agent in the "before" picture. There is no other divine-like agent or monstrous force that is before or outside God's creative intent. There is nothing "outside the house" threatening to intrude. In a profound twist, monsters are *part of* the world. "God created the great sea monsters" (Gen. 1:21, NRSV). In a similar perspective, Psalm 104:25–26 says, "There is the sea, vast and spacious, teeming with creatures beyond number—living things both large and small. There the ships go to and fro, and Leviathan, which you formed to frolic there." This imagery should give us pause. In the whole of this narrative, God has been working for the sake of an otherwise dead, empty earth. There has been the gift of God's Spirit and Word for the world's good. God's graciousness has opened up for the world the possibility of productive responsiveness. Each feature of creation is directed *for* the well-being of other things and the welfare of the community. Yet here, for the good, this Creator makes

---

13. Beal, *Religion and Its Monsters*, 5. What is fascinating is that, for several thousand years in Mesopotamian cultures, they gave the title "great dragon" to the god(s) who defeated the primal forces and to their greatest kings (Yoder, "Ezekiel 29:3," 490f.).

the monstrous—what is different, unpredictable, unsettling, dangerous—*within* and *of* the world.

One thing the Torah teaches about God—even in all of God's dependability—is that God is "not like a tame lion" (as C. S. Lewis writes of Aslan in *The Lion, the Witch and the Wardrobe*). God's very name is "I AM WHO I AM," or "I WILL BE WHAT I WILL BE" (Exod. 3:14). Humankind can negotiate and wrestle with God, but humankind will not (indeed, cannot) script for God the course God must take.[14] At the same time, creation has in itself this wildness too— what we experience as the monstrous. The world is not a tame lion. God gifts to the world God's creative intentions, and there is a certain sense of dependability in the world's response, but life is also not predictable or safe. God does not script this world, and the world does not always express itself in ways that line up with divine intentions; there can be taking of life instead of fostering it, laying waste instead of cultivation. Distinction between God and creation carries with it that the two parties have their own integrity to express themselves and not script the other. There is an important implication here. Just as we should not read the heavenly bodies, we should also not look at every natural disaster either as God's action to be interpreted or indication that our Creator is facing a serious challenger (see, for example, Job 41). If there are monsters in the water, some things that happen in the world are sens*eless*. There is no logic at work in every disaster to be found, no law of creation at work in them, no meaning that can be made of

---

14. See, for example, Walter Brueggemann's commentary on Exodus 32-34 ("The Book of Exodus," *The New Interpreter's Bible, Volume* 1 (Nashville: Abingdon, 1994). Also, note that Israel's sacrificial system was not a system of contractual exchange or a mechanism for controlling God's response. It was a space for interpersonally relating between God and creature. God remained free, and any response from God was a gift, not an obligation (see Vail, *Atonement and Salvation*, 77-86, 92-96, and 150f., n. 6).

them. While the Scriptures promise that God ultimately will bring together the heavens and the earth in the glory of God's purposes, God has called forth a world that, in all its vibrancy of life, carries in it features of the monstrous.

In this text, the monsters are *in* the sea, but the sea itself is not a monster. This distinction is another key difference from Israel's neighbors. Where some of them believed the very materials of the world were remnants of a primordial enemy—like the slain Tiamat and her general—Genesis does not teach that creation is God's adversary or an adversarial substance. The waters in Genesis 1 respond in a positive way to God's farming. No doubt, there are instances in the Torah when God uses the waters for the purpose of delivering judgment against evildoers—to flood the earth or destroy Egypt's army (Gen. 7:11; Exod. 14:15–31). Even then, however, the waters operate as a faithful subject according to God's purposes. According to these Torah texts, the waters themselves are not a monstrous agent acting independently from or against God's will.[15] Some passages in the Old Testament's Writings and Prophets depict the seas

---

15. Even a scholar who views waters in the Bible as a force of chaos notes that God uses those same waters "to enact his judgment upon the wicked (Gen. 7:11), including his own people (e.g., Isa. 8:7)" (Angel, *Chaos and the Son of Man*, 19). The waters are under God's dominion. Outside the area of monsters, Anne Marie Kitz has done research into the idea of the demonic in the writings of Israel and the ancient Near East ("Demons in the Hebrew Bible and the Ancient Near East," *JBL* 135, no. 3 [2016]: 447–64). Out of her investigations, she concludes that "demons as inherently evil subordinate supernatural beings did not exist in the ancient Near East. They are, rather, divinely articulated verdicts handed down as judgments in response to human transgressions" (447). In other words, the subordinate beings served a mediating function from divinity to creatures—not making the being itself evil. It is simply the bearer of bad news. For example, "the evil spirit of God" in 1 Samuel 16:15 is a spirit produced by God's "windy words that express his judgment against wayward human behavior." It is not that evil is a characteristic of either God's very being or this spirit from God, but the evil "refers to the character of the event articulated in the divine message" (448). In a similar way, the waters of Genesis 1 are not inherently evil, even if they were used to mediate God's judgment against human transgression in the flood or against the Egyptian army at the Red Sea. God even used various nations to

as monstrous or destructive, but that is a different perspective than what Genesis 1 gives.[16]

Knowing that the monstrous—the different, illogical, or destructive—is not an outside threat but is *part of* creation itself may have other implications. In other cultures, agents who were monstrous to them or represented what could never belong in their god's world should be barred from entry or participation *in* the world. Some of their religious practices were magic-like in warding off intrusions from those outside forces that were horrifyingly foreign or disruptive. Thus, their whole system enabled a distinction between what did and did not belong in their god's order of things. They had a category of things (or agents) that were, *by nature*, to be cut off from their world. They could imagine something being excluded, by virtue that it existed before and outside their god's intentions, care, and blessings. In contrast, nothing in Israel's creation account is, *by nature*, outside of God's world; therefore, nothing is outside of God's loving provision. Certainly in the Torah, Israel learned what things are *for* within God's governance. Some animals and animal parts are *for* eating; some are not. Some ways of treating the world and its inhabitants are right; some are not. Some people follow God's pathways of righteousness; others do not. Exclusion from the world or from Israel's life was on the basis of what something or someone *did* in relation to God's governing ways, not because of what something or someone *was* by nature or divine purpose. There was to be room in the promised land and at Israel's table for any foreigner to join the blessings

---

mediate judgment against other nations—sometimes even against Israel. Such a function does not make any of those nations inherently or fundamentally evil.

16. Watson's *Chaos Uncreated* gives a careful, detailed examination of waters in the OT and is worth consulting.

that flowed out of Torah life.[17] Hospitality is written into the Torah.

The flow of Genesis 1 challenged many of the beliefs held by Israel's neighbors. There were no primal male and female principles that birth the major gods. The various features of the world—the major elements—were not divine or divine-like. God did not come from or draw strength from any preceding thing. Rather, all things were blessed with God's own life-nurturing activity. The sun, moon, and stars were not divine or to be decoded as messages from the divine realm.[18] There also were not extra-divine forces (monsters) trying to break into the world, threatening God's creative purposes. In Genesis, God is the maker of all there is, visible and invisible. All things are ultimately under and within God's domain—even if they are not scripted or functioning according to divine purposes.[19] So much of what Israel's neighbors imagined was divine or an exten-

---

17. Not only was Israel to host people who came to them from outside their covenant patterns (since they could not be considered outside of God's creative care), but Israel also had to establish a network of cities in order to accommodate manslayers in their midst—people guilty of the horror of accidental killing (see Eric Severson, *Scandalous Obligation: Rethinking Christian Responsibility* [Kansas City, MO: Beacon Hill Press of Kansas City, 2011], 70–83). Jesus took this so far as to tell his followers to love their enemies and pray for their persecutors. His followers cannot hate or hold grudges. They cannot have a posture toward another person that cuts any part of God's creation out of the believers' world (or responsibility). The practice of Christians is not only to forgive others but also to confess their own sins. The monster amid God's provisions for the world is us. We too run crossways to God's purposes, just as people who are outsiders to us. Every outsider is still and always God's insider—God's creation.

18. The heavenly bodies were also not going to help in performing magic to hold off or call upon outside evil forces; see Daniel Schwemer, "Gods & Stars," Julius-Maximilians-Universität Würzburg (2014), http://www.cmawro.altorientalistik.uni-wuerzburg.de/magic-witchcraft/gods-stars/.

19. For example, there were three different famines recorded in Genesis (12:10; 26:1; 41:27–36). Yet God's activity is not in the famine but "to save lives . . . to preserve for you a remnant on earth and to save your lives by a great deliverance" (Gen. 45:5, 7). God began that salvation in advance through Joseph's life story.

sion of divine activity, Genesis 1 makes into a common part of creation, subject to the only God.

Day 6

On this final day of the parallel structure, the land was populated. Back on day 3, dry ground appeared when the waters gathered together (Gen. 1:9). In the ground's function as land, it was to produce vegetation (v. 11). This was not a once-upon-a-time, one-and-done action. The land was perpetually to produce—or "to grass grass," like the waters were "to swarm swarmers."[20] It is an ongoing vocation. Just like making music requires continued activity, the land has an enduring function. Even its produce is to have the same character of perpetual provision—"seed-bearing plants" and trees bearing "fruit with seed in it" (v. 11; see Joel 2:22). The land's own fertility supports reproductive vegetation. God's creative blessings to the land on day 3 make the land a blessing to its day-6 inhabitants. Its bountiful produce will feed all the land-dwellers (Gen. 1:29–30; see Ps. 104:5–18).

Just as the waters were called to support the life of swimmers and flyers (Gen. 1:20), so the land is called to support walkers and crawlers. "Let the land produce living creatures according to their kinds" (v. 24). The land in this text is neither a natural resource *for* human purposes nor merely a background for the story. The land is called by our Creator to fulfill a role in supporting animal life, beyond just producing its food. The animals it supports are of every category: walking and ground-hugging, farm and wild. The full spectrum of animal-kind is included within God's creative purposes. They are all included under divine blessing for the life of the world.

---

20. The idea of "grass" as a verb in Hebrew is from Robert D. Sacks, *A Commentary on the Book of Genesis* (Lewiston, NY: E. Mellen Press, 1990), 7. Sacks also makes the connection to Joel 2:22—the only other place "grass" is used as a verb.

The creation of humankind marks both similarity and dissimilarity in the text. On the one hand, day 6 keeps the pattern of populating realms; day 3 deals with the realm of the land and food, and day 6 deals with the air-breathing creatures that inhabit the land and eat the food. Humans share this day with fellow creatures.[21] Also, in parallel with day 3, day 6 also has two creative calls. Day 3 had calls for dry ground (v. 9) and vegetation (v. 11). Day 6 has animals (v. 24) and humans (v. 26).

On the other hand, there is a break in the pattern. God had called to the water and land in order to prepare these spaces to support inhabitants (vv. 9, 11). God called to the water and the land to host swimmers, flyers, walkers, and crawlers (vv. 20, 24). With humans, for the first time in the creation of a living creature, God does not call to the water or the land. God's call is self-referential: "Let us make humankind" (v. 26, NRSV). So much ink has been spilled evaluating the plural pronoun "us." Whether it points in advance to God's triune nature or is a royal "we," we should not lose what this pattern break might be saying about the divine-human relationship. Certainly within the narrative structure, humans are a sixth-day creature; they are an air-breathing, land-treading, plant-eating creature (vv. 29–30). Yet, in their creation, the *domain* established on day 3 is not addressed. God takes this creation personally. Even while our life is earthbound, God is the *domain* in whom and out of whom we are to function (see Acts 17:28a).

---

21. John Muir reflected, "The man of science, the naturalist, too often loses sight of the essential oneness of all living beings in seeking to classify them in kingdoms, orders, species, etc. While the eye of the poet, the seer, never closes on the kinship of all God's creatures and his heart ever beats in sympathy with great and small alike, as earth-born companions and fellow mortals, equally dependent on heaven's eternal love" (quoted in "The Last Refuge (1890–1915)," *The National Parks: America's Best Idea*, 1:40:07–1:40:44).

No feature of the world has been called to function for itself or self-interest. Every feature functions for the flourishing of the whole community of creation.

This special relation of humankind with God is the necessary condition for humans to function as the image and likeness of God (Gen. 1:26). So many theories have circulated about what "image" and "likeness" could mean: we look like God, we have higher-level intellect, we have divine-like capacities or qualities, etc. So often these theories focus on something we *are* or *possess* in our substance—thus, a tangible, fixed *thing* that can be lost, damaged, or destroyed. However, we should keep in mind the historical context. With the authority to create, God is introducing divine purposes for the functionality of this kingdom (i.e., the economy of the world). The *creation* of humankind means the communication of divine purpose for us—what we are *for*. Humankind is meant to image creation's Creator in ruling (v. 26). *Image* points toward our function (our calling); it is more of an action or verb than a thing or noun. It is God's purpose *for* us, based out of our special abiding in God. We are not created to be God for the heavens and the earth. God alone creates (*bara*); we are not co-creators, or replacement creators. We are meant to reflect the only one who is Ruler-Creator-Redeemer, creation's Beginning and End. Divine purposes are not meant to originate with us but only be reflected in our operation—in image and likeness.

This purpose, then, colors all sense about what it means for humankind to "rule." God has not ruled (created) out of self-interest or benefit. Rather, God has been giving God's self in Spirit and Word for the world's own flourishing. In turn, every feature of the world has reflected the self-giving of God within the world as it serves its purpose toward a full, thriving world. No feature has been called to function for itself or self-interest. Every feature functions for the benefit of something else and, thus, the flourishing of the whole community of creation. God did not create the world *for* humans any more than God created it *for* Godself. Humans were created *for* the world as much as God has been working *for* the world. We dare not rewrite what we—or any features of creation—are for. It is all *for* shining the character of the self-giving, other-blessing Creator.

Human rule (our vocation) reflects our Creator's. We are to "rule over the fish in the sea and the birds in the sky, over the livestock and all the wild animals, and over all the creatures that move along the ground" (v. 26). We are to "fill the earth and subdue it" (v. 28). All these tasks should be according to the image and likeness of God and God's purposes for these things—helping them flourish in their vocations. Like God, we do not labor in our own vocation for personal profit or benefit. We do not get to consume anything we rule; it is not *for* us. The only thing we get to consume is vegetation that is lovingly given to us by God and the land, out of the fertile land and reproducing plants (vv. 29–30).

One final issue about humankind: it is not a single human that is created to image God. Israel's neighbors had stories of their kings being the image of divinity in the world. That lone *male* figure held that distinction. The rest of humanity was created in a lower status. By the will of their creator, the masses were meant to be ruled and to serve the one who himself imaged their self-interested gods. Genesis 1 has an audacious counterclaim to this cultural norm. Instead of a lone male figure, all of *humankind* images God. It is not a lone person who can do such a thing. (Perhaps this reality is indicated in the plural, "Let us.") We are not each, on our own, the image of God. Humankind together is meant to fulfill this role as they increase in number and fill the earth (v. 28). Even more, it is neither male nor female that can image God apart from the other. God is neither male nor female. It is the breadth of humankind— the whole array *from* male *to* female—who only together can offer a wide enough likeness of God. Only the totality of all gendered humanity can approximate an image of God in its work.

It Was Good

"Good" in the Old Testament is not the same as in the Greek philosophical tradition, where it is more like an eternally fixed ideal that things more or less represent.[22] Instead, the functional nature of creative activity (*bara*) helps us understand the affirmation that something was "good" (*tob*, or *tov*). Six times in the narrative, "God saw that it was good" (Gen. 1:4, 10, 12, 18, 21, 25); the seventh time "God saw all that he had made, and it was very good" (v. 31).

"Good" (*tob*) was used in Israel's writings a number of ways.[23] First, "good" could mean something had a practical benefit or was good *for* something; it was suitable.[24] For the purpose of driving nails, a hammer is *good*. Second, it could mean something fits our preference or will—so a "good egg" would be one prepared according to our liking. Third, it would be possible to indicate our agreement or acceptance of something with "good"—a form of signing off. Fourth, "good" could indicate a pleasant appearance ("looks good") or one's happiness ("all is good"). Lastly, there was moral goodness; we are to "*do* good" to our neighbor.[25]

---

22. W. Grundmann, "ἀγαθός, ἀγαθοεργέω, ἀγαθοποιέω, -ός, -ία, ἀγαθωσύνη, φιλάγαθος, ἀφιλάγαθος," *Theological Dictionary of the New Testament, Vol. 1*, ed. G. Kittel, G. W. Bromiley, & G. Friedrich, (Grand Rapids: Eerdmans, 1964), 13. Even in the way the Septuagint used the Greek word for "good" (*agathos*) to translate the Hebrew word for "good" (*tob*), "the idea of the good in the Greek and Hellenistic sense is not present" (Grundmann, 13).

23. The following list is drawn from A. Bowling, "793 טוב," *Theological Wordbook of the Old Testament*, ed. R. L. Harris, G. L. Archer Jr, and B. K. Waltke (Chicago: Moody Press, 1999), 345.

24. Walton takes this view (*The Lost World of Genesis One*, 149–51).

25. Jenson leans in the direction of morality (*Systematic Theology, Volume 2: The Works of God*, 8). He sees *bara* as conveying God's "moral intentions."

In Hebrew, more than one sense of "good" could be implied in a single use of the word *tob*. It would be hard in Genesis 1 to narrow down God's assessment to only one sense of "good." Perhaps on the various days, God was affirming that what God intended in God's call(s) would be fulfilled adequately with the response that came from creation. Perhaps God was accepting creation's unfolding, seeing that it was good for the flourishing God intended. Perhaps God was happy, admiring the world's beauty. Given that God's intent was that all things would act for the good of other things in the world, there may also have been a moral goodness that God was seeing at work in the world. When both sets of three days were completed, God's seventh, fullest expression of "good" was given in regard to the total heavens and earth: "it was very good" (v. 31).

We may be tempted to think that life on the earth is a hindrance to living out God's purposes. However, Genesis 1 teaches the opposite. God affirms and delights in the reality that life in creation is good—in the heavens *and the earth*. The world, cultivated and enlivened by God's Spirit and Word, is the very good domain of its loving Creator. It is a domain God blesses to be alive in accordance with God's own self-giving, other-nurturing love. What God purposed for the world from the beginning is creation's destiny. God will bring to everlasting fulfillment what God started.

Day 7

We should not cut off day 7 from the preceding two sets of three days (days 1 through 6). Day 7 is the climactic claim toward which the whole narrative has moved; it is implicit in the days leading up to this day. It is the flashing neon light in the narrative space. It is not a day tacked on, in which nothing is happening. Rather, "without hesitation the ancient reader would conclude that . . . day seven is the most important of the seven days."²⁶ If the whole of creation is *for* something, this is it! It is the meaning and point toward which the whole narrative has moved. Just as in the book of Exodus, much of the narrative is given to the Israelites building the tabernacle in the wilderness (Exod. 25–39), but the grand finale was when it came to be inhabited by God (Exod. 40). In a parallel way, the bulk of Genesis 1 is God building a sanctuary in days 1 to 6. The part that should make our hearts soar and have us fall on our faces is God resting in the sanctuary on day 7.

The magnitude of what Genesis 1 communicates on day 7 may become clearer when we learn how the Babylonians' Enuma Elish ends. After Marduk arranged the heavens and earth, he went back to the assembly of gods and made a declaration that he would build a temple for himself in the city of Babylon, next to the shared temple he built for the gods. That would place Marduk's temple at the center of creation, above the waters of the deep and below the heavens above. Marduk's shrine would be in his temple. Thus, his temple would serve as his centralized kingly chamber, in which all the gods would come to *rest* in the divine assembly for the sake of making any decisions. Once Marduk finished his speech, he hatched a plan to make the gods build his temple for him. Marduk placed them in his debt, and they responded to Marduk as he contrived. They said to him, "Now, lord, seeing you have established our freedom, what favour can we do for you? Let us make a shrine of great renown: your chamber will be our resting place wherein we may repose. Let us erect a shrine to house a pedestal wherein we may repose when we finish (the work)." When they were finished, they all sat down "in the lofty shrine which they had built for his dwelling, (saying,)

---

26. Walton, *The Lost World of Genesis One*, 72.

'This is Babylon, your fixed dwelling, take your pleasure here! Sit down in joy!'"[27]

In the ancient Near East it was typical for a temple to be built *at the end* of a creation narrative in which the creator-god could reside in the world. Genesis 1 makes a profound claim through what is *missing* from the narrative. God did not build a temple when "the heavens and the earth were completed in all their vast array" (Gen. 2:1). *Days 1 through 6 were God's construction of God's temple.* As Isaiah wrote, "This is what the Lord says: 'Heaven is my throne, and the earth is my footstool. Where is the house you will build for me? Where will my resting place be? Has not my hand made all these things, and so they came into being?' declares the Lord" (Isa. 66:1–2). The work of creating (*bara*) is the work of the Creator-Ruler setting precedent for all the subjects of the kingdom. The fitting conclusion would be for God to preside in the kingdom. "The Lord has established his throne in heaven, and his kingdom rules over all. . . . Praise the Lord, all his works everywhere in his dominion" (Ps. 103:19, 22; see 1 Kings 8:27–30; Pss. 11:4; 93:1–5). God was present from even before creation as the Spirit hovered (Gen. 1:2). Amid the Spirit's presence, God's call went out, beckoning lively response. A sanctuary space reflecting God's gracious dominion unfolded. On day 7, God was at home in the sanctuary.[28]

---

27. Enuma Elish, Tablet V:118–130; Tablet VI:1–2, 45–73, https://www.ancient.eu/article/225/enuma-elish—-the-babylonian-epic-of-creation—-fu/.

28. In other words, "Gen. 1 is not intended to present a summary of the material origins of the earth, or of any of the rest of the cosmos: *What* all did God make? *How* did God make it? *When* did God make it? Rather, the purpose of Gen. 1 is to report the *functional* beginnings of the earth, its systems, and its creatures, as God's cosmic temple. That is, Gen. 1 reports the inauguration of the earth as God's dwelling place, from which God directs and superintends the *functions* of the various entities and systems" (Coleson, *Genesis 1–11*, 38; Coleson is describing and agreeing with Walton's position in *The Lost World of Genesis One*, 38–46).

The connection between the whole creation and Israel's sanctuary spaces is present throughout Israel's writings. In God's relationship with Israel, God had them build a tabernacle in which God dwelt during their time in the wilderness and the early settlement of Canaan. God gave the instructions for the tabernacle in seven units, the last of which was an instruction to keep the Sabbath (Exod. 25–31). Later, God allowed Solomon to build a temple in Jerusalem as God's special resting place; it took Solomon seven years to complete it, and it was dedicated in the seventh month during a seven-day festival (1 Kings 6:38; see Ps. 132:7–8, 13–14).[29] The connection between Israel's sanctuaries and all creation being a sanctuary in Genesis 1 goes beyond the number seven. The two sets of three days in Genesis 1 follow the arrangement of Israel's sanctuaries.[30] The temple was entered from the east, where the sun rises. Since it was covered in gold, the rising sun reflected brilliantly into the eyes of those who entered.[31] Genesis 1 opens each set of three days with light and lights. One function of those lights was to mark sacred times, to order rhythms of special observances (v. 14). Upon entering

---

29. Jon D. Levenson, *Creation and the Persistence of Evil: The Jewish Drama of Divine Omnipotence* (San Francisco: Harper & Row, 1988), 78. See also Levenson, *Sinai & Zion: An Entry into the Jewish Bible* (San Francisco: Harper & Row, 1987), 143–145; and Brown, "Divine Act and the Art of Persuasion in Genesis 1," 29–30.

30. For a virtual tour of Solomon's temple, see "Solomon's Temple," https://youtu.be/oiF-wObznds. Scholars have been noting for some time how the structure of Genesis 1 follows the structure of a sanctuary. See, for example, Brown, *Seven Pillars of Creation*, 36–44; and Walton, *The Lost World of Genesis One*, 72–85.

31. Josephus, a first-century-AD Jewish historian, described this experience: "Now the outward face of the temple in its front wanted nothing that was likely to surprise either men's minds or their eyes; for it was covered all over with plates of gold of great weight, and, at the first rising of the sun, reflected back a very fiery splendor, and made those who forced themselves to look upon it to turn their eyes away, just as they would have done at the sun's own rays" (*The Wars of the Jews, Or The History of the Destruction of Jerusalem*, Book 5, Chapter 5, Section 6, https://www.sacred-texts.com/jud/josephus/war-5.htm).

the temple, there was then an open-air courtyard with the bronze sea and ten basins of water. In Genesis 1, the second day in each set deals with the heavenly dome and waters of the earth, along with their inhabitants. The final day in each set of three deals with the land, food, and land inhabitants. The actual temple building had an entrance supported by two massive pillars. The decorations on the pillars and the building were plants—pomegranates, palm trees, and flowers. Inside there was also a table with bread on it—food from the land.

Here is a diagram to help with visualizing the link between the structure of Genesis 1 and Solomon's temple in 1 Kings 6–8.[32]

---

32. Interestingly, in Enuma Elish, the temple the gods built for Marduk was a replica of the watery deep (Apsu), with Marduk's throne sitting as the land does at the peak above the waters (Tablet VI:59–66). Levenson notes Egypt's connection of their temples with the earth. They believed the land rose up out of the primordial waters. So "ultimately every temple which had a high place for its god probably considered that high place to be the place of creation." They could even imagine that a pharaoh buried in a pyramid (hill) would "emerge again into new being"—like a new creation (*Creation and the Persistence of Evil*, 74). Israel made connections between creation and their temples through architecture and the number seven. "If these temples were constructed in terms of 'seven,' it is really no wonder that the creation poem of Gen. 1 is inserted in a seven-day framework. One must speak of ordering the cosmos in terms of seven even as the construction of the microcosm must be according to the sacred number" (Levenson quoting Loren Fisher, *Creation and the Persistence of Evil*, 79). Both tabernacle-sanctuary and creation were according to God's instruction. "Collectively, the function of these correspondences is to underscore the depiction of the sanctuary as a world, that is, an ordered, supportive, and obedient environment, and the depiction of the world as a sanctuary, that is, a place in which the reign of God is visible and unchallenged, and his holiness is palpable, unthreatened, and pervasive" (Levenson, 86).

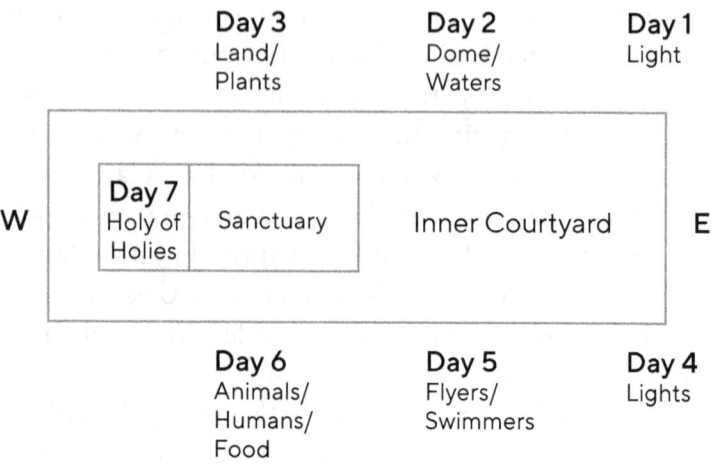

God inhabits God's creation as God inhabited the sanctuaries of Israel. Creation is intended to be God's dwelling place, a place of shared fellowship of God with all God's creation. Day 7 has no parallel in Genesis 1. Indeed, *God* has no parallel. Day 7 is the heart of the temple, where God's presence dwells in the midst of it all.[33]

Genesis says, "By the seventh day God had finished the work he had been doing; so on the seventh day he rested from all his work" (2:2). Perhaps the significance of this has not captured us because it sounds like God took a nap and we are just peeking in on a sleeping God. However, we can note from the Enuma Elish that the ancient Near East saw "rest" as the condition for normal operations and decision-making. Now that all the norms had been worked out (days 1–6), it was possible to "settle down" in the sta-

---

33. When Solomon's temple was built on Mount Zion in Jerusalem, Israel imagined that Zion was the navel of creation, "the point from which creation proceeded." The temple was also imagined as the "'point of junction between heaven, earth, and hell.' . . . [It] is a kind of fulcrum for the universe" (Levenson, *Sinai & Zion*, 116, 122). As Josephus wrote, the temple building had no doors, "for it represented the universal visibility of heaven, and that it cannot be excluded from any place" (*Wars of the Jews* 5.5.4, https://www.sacred-texts.com/jud/josephus/war-5.htm).

bility.³⁴ Israel too would enjoy "rest" in the promised land, when everyone would stop "doing as they see fit" (Deut. 12:8) and do "what is good and right in the eyes of the Lord your God" (v. 28). They were instructed to "settle in the land the Lord your God is giving you as an inheritance, and he will give you rest from all your enemies around you so that you will live in safety" (v. 10).³⁵ An era of rest in the life of the people was not an era of sleep; it was an era of peace and stability. It would be like the period after moving into a new home when the last box is unpacked and everything is put in its place. Everything is very good. The space is equipped for living; it is home.

Sabbath days and Sabbath years were God's gift to Israel to join in a rhythm that rests in the sufficiency of all that God has ordained. Through rest, we affirm the goodness of God's creation. We can be content settling into the way God has called it to function. We are also participating in blessing those around us as we stop and share with the world the bounty from our loving Redeemer-Creator-Ruler's dominion.

All space, all time, and all activity in the world is sacred. The whole of it is *from* the Lord (a gift) and *unto* the Lord (to all of our delight in the richness of this communion). As I have written elsewhere, in making creation as God's sanctuary dwelling, God is calling into being, joining, partnering with, and finding a dwelling place in the fellowship of a community God self-gifts to enjoy the love God has in God's own self as Father, Son, and Holy Spirit. The shared life that Genesis 1 teaches shines (glorifies) the very face of our Redeemer-Creator-Ruler. The life of the world is a living testament to the character of God and God's purposes with us and for us. God's full presence and

---

34. Walton, *The Lost World of Genesis One*, 73.
35. Walton, *The Lost World of Genesis One*, 74.

our fulfillment in God's blessing for the world's life are creation's destiny (see Rev. 21–22). All glory, honor, and praise be unto the Father, Son, and Holy Spirit, now and forever!

Message of Assurance

Remember our earlier discussion about how many scholars date the writing of Genesis 1 to the time of Israel's exile, when their homeland lay desolate and emptied (Isa. 45:18; Jer. 4:23–29; Ezek. 36:3–5). The people themselves felt dead; in their captivity they said, "Our bones are dried up and our hope is gone; we are cut off" (Ezek. 37:11). They had failed to walk in the ways of the Lord so that they would flourish in the richness of God's promises and intentions for them. They had done the opposite of walk in God's ways and be a blessing to others. Instead they walked in the ways of idols and "shed blood in the land" (Ezek. 36:18).

In their desolation and captivity, they had no capacity in themselves to overturn their situation. They saw no hope and no future for themselves. The God who had delivered them and established them before would have to do that again. God would have to renew and restore the land, making it ready to receive inhabitants (Ezek. 36:8–12, 29–36). The Spirit of God would have to move across the people to revive them (Ezek. 37:6, 8–10, 14). God would have to cleanse and recreate the people and make them ready to live rightly in the land (Ezek. 36:22–28; 36:37–37:28). The climactic result of God's restoration of the land and the people—both environment and inhabitants—would be God's dwelling in their midst. As God spoke through the prophet Ezekiel, "I will establish them and increase their numbers, and I will put my sanctuary among them forever. My dwelling place will be with them; I will be their God, and they will be my people. Then the nations will know that I the Lord make Israel holy, when my sanctuary is among them forever" (Ezek. 37:26–28; see Ezek. 40–48).

The salvation narrative of the prophets is paralleled in the creation narrative of Genesis 1.

As Israel lived in exile among the traditions of their captors, they trusted the prophets' words of comfort and promise. They could have believed that the disasters that swept over them were primeval monsters intruding into the world. They could have believed the gods of their captors were real and greater than God. They could have believed the nations, who said Israel and their God were nothing. Yet they affirmed that God was indeed Creator of all there is. They affirmed that God is the only divine power in all the world. The gods of the nations were nothing but wood and stone figures (Isa. 37:19; 45:20; Jer. 2:27; Ezek. 20:32), and the created order was a faithful subject under God's rule. God alone had acted against them, and no other powers (Isa. 45:7, 20–25). God had been right to act in judgment; they violated the covenant. The nature of God's creative activity from the dawn of creation was the very thing God would do in their midst now. They could have confidence that the One who is Creator could and would accomplish their redemption. God's redemptive work would recreate the people and the land back into the life-giving pathways of God.

Israel's creation beliefs helped focus their vision of God and the world in their time of crisis. Their reflections helped clarify God's character, God's care for the world, and God's purposes for creation. Their theological work also helped deconstruct the world their neighbors imagined. The world is meant to respond to its Redeemer-Creator-Ruler and is not made of divine actors. Genesis 1 is a thorough rejection of the beliefs of Israel's neighbors and captors. It affirms that Israel's faithful Redeemer is Creator in a manner consistent with everything God said and did in Israel's history. Israel and all creation had God alone to turn to, to fear, to trust, and to obey. And God's rule is a blessing for all when the glory of our Creator rests in this place. "The earth is filled with your love, LORD; teach me your decrees" (Ps. 119:64).

Conclusion

Genesis 1, this opening passage of the Torah, is to be a lamp lighting our path in every moment and every place. It ought to frame our imagination of God and the world we inhabit. We can know what the world is for, its God-given vocation. We can know our own vocation as contributors in this economy of self-giving for the benefit of others. We can know that we are not here to be served but to serve.

This is not a text that should sit a long way off in our imaginations, as simply the first days in history. It should also not be treated as historical or scientific data. As Torah, it is not really functioning as precise historical fact. It is, rather, to guide our living. It is the truth about God and God's ways for us. In a similar vein, it is not a twenty-first-century scientific text. It reflects the scientific understanding of the ancient Near East, and it works within that framework for the purpose of teaching theology and shaping faithful living. From end to end it teaches truth while communicating effectively in the ancient understanding of the world and its method of narrating a creation story.

I hope our own journey through Genesis 1 has illuminated its theology and brought it into our imagination for daily living. May we and all creation live in and to the glory of our Creator!

FIVE

Old Testament Voices

One tendency among Christians has been to look at Genesis 1 as *the* biblical statement on creation (maybe including Genesis 2 as well). I have likely fueled that tendency in this book by starting with that text and devoting the most attention to it. Genesis 1 certainly has the privilege of being the first word we read in the Bible on the topic. Its age also places it among the last capstone statements made on the topic in the Old Testament.

Nevertheless, Genesis 1 is not the totality of everything the Old Testament has to say about Creator and creation. There are other texts in the Bible that give us different viewpoints.[1] We have already noted that the prophets from around the time of Israel's exile turned to the topic of creation in order to affirm that God can and would redeem Israel. Toward that goal, Isaiah 40–55 has far more uses of the Hebrew term *bara* ("create") than any other biblical text. Other significant passages that teach about the Creator and/or creation include Genesis 2, Psalm 104, Job 38–41, Proverbs 8, and Ecclesiastes.[2] This list by no means

---

1. Several books have been written that explore the breadth of Old Testament perspectives on creation, including *God Who Creates*, ed. William P. Brown and S. Dean McBride Jr. (2000); and Brown's *The Seven Pillars of Creation* (2010).

2. The varying way that different scholars view Psalms makes it difficult to cover here. Some scholars view many psalms as references to God's initial creative activities. Those creation references, like Psalms 44, 74, 77, 80 and 89 are the basis for hope in crisis (Clifford, "*Creatio ex nihilo* in the Old Testament/He-

exhausts the whole array of Old Testament perspectives. Some texts deal with a specific part of creation. For example, Job 10 and Psalm 139 each address individual people as God's creation.³

This chapter does not unpack these many perspectives with the same detailed approach as was taken with Genesis 1. The aim instead is to lay out points of emphasis that these texts have about God and creation, which will help us see some of the diversity and complexity in the Bible's teaching. Yet, even with the diversity, God as Ruler remains the dominant view of God's creative role.

Genesis 2

Not every creation narrative considers the whole breadth of created things like Genesis 1 does. Some of them emphasize pieces of the world. The focus of Genesis 2 is humankind. If we look at the broader narrative unit of chapters 2–4, we see an account of God's intention for humankind next to the dynamics of how humans actually live. We see this in the contrast between the fullness of life in the garden of Eden and the hardscrabble life outside the garden.⁴

---

brew Bible," 68). However, instead of seeing these as references to a primal time that leads to the dawn of creation, other scholars see these psalms as references to mighty acts of salvation—like Israel's deliverance from Egypt at the Red Sea (Watson, *Chaos Uncreated*). Certainly such mighty acts create new circumstances for Israel and can fall under the Hebrew term *bara* ("create"). Scholars differ over which creative event is referenced in some of these psalms. The same issue is at play in passages like Isaiah 43:16–21 and 51:9–11 (compare Exod. 15:1–21). Exodus (salvation) and creation imagery are interwoven since both actions are included within God's *creative* work (see Clifford, "Creatio ex nihilo," 70–71); for example, in Genesis 1 and Exodus 14, wind moves over waters, and waters move so dry land appears.

3. See Brown, "*Creatio corporis* and the Rhetoric of Defense in Job 10 and Psalm 139," *God Who Creates*, 107–24.

4. For more of what I have written about Genesis 2, see "Creation and Human Vocation," *Atonement and Salvation*; and "Background Check" and "The Narrative's Arc," *Eschatology* (Kansas City, MO: The Foundry Publishing, 2020).

While Genesis 2 turns our attention to humankind, it is not entirely disconnected from Genesis 1. The transition in 2:4—between the narratives of Genesis 1 and 2—weaves the two passages together. On one hand, the transition can be read as the end of the Genesis 1 account: "This is the account of [*toledot*] the heavens and the earth when they were created [*bara*]." This is the seventh appearance of *bara* in Genesis, which is why many scholars say the Genesis 1 account runs from Genesis 1:1–2:4a. However, on the other hand, 2:4 also moves readers into the Genesis 2 narrative by using a common introductory statement in Genesis: "this is the story of" (*toledot*). Either way, the editors of Genesis did well stitching the two narratives together. Even though scholars commonly believe the two texts had different authors with different viewpoints, word preferences, and plotlines, it is possible to see harmony between them.[5] It can be viewed as further clarification of day 6, during which God created humankind, male and female, in God's image and blessed them to be fruitful and fill the earth and subdue it (Gen. 1:27–28).

One of the most significant points of agreement Genesis 2 has with Genesis 1 is that the world is meant to serve as God's sanctuary. The garden of Eden described in Genesis 2 is connected with imagery that is used across the Old Testament to portray the Jerusalem temple.[6] Like portrayals of the temple, a river flowed out from Eden to provide life-giv-

---

5. Coleson shows in *Genesis 1–11* the way Genesis 1 and 2 can be read together, explaining that not all the tensions highlighted by previous scholars are necessary conclusions from the text's wording or verb tenses. Hebrew does not have verb tenses specific enough to make it clear whether Genesis 2 has a different sequence of events than Genesis 1—like in which order animals and humans are made. In contrast, other scholars suggest that the Genesis 2 narrative "cannot be harmonized with the earlier passage through any amount of exegetical ingenuity" (Clifford, "*Creatio ex nihilo*," 66).

6. Gordon Wenham, "Sanctuary Symbolism in the Garden of Eden Story," *I Studied Inscriptions from before the Flood*, 399–404. Or, as Steven Tuell notes about Israelite belief, even beyond literary imagery, "it is clear that Zion and

ing water far and wide (Gen. 2:10–14; Ezek. 47).[7] Eden's entrance faces east (Gen. 3:24; Num. 2:3; 3:38). The precious materials mentioned in the narrative were used to construct the temple and priestly garments (Gen. 2:11–12). Like the sanctuary, God walks with people there (Gen. 3:8; Lev. 26:12; Deut. 23:15). The people's role was to "tend and keep" the garden, as priests were to do with the temple (Gen. 2:15; Exod. 3:12; Num. 28:2). Cherubim guard both places (Gen. 3:24; Exod. 36:8; 37:9). Even details about the tree of life and the tree of the knowledge of good and evil can be associated with Israel's sanctuary spaces and keeping the covenant (see Exod. 25:16, 31–40; Num. 4:20; Ps. 19:7–13).[8]

One effect of linking the garden of Eden with Israel's heritage of sanctuaries and covenant is that this Torah narrative illustrates to readers the difference between following the paths of obedience and disobedience (see Deut. 11 and 28). One path is full of blessings; the other is cursed. As Moses said to the Israelites, "The LORD is your life," and the way God was calling them to live was for the sake of "life and prosperity" (Deut. 30:15, 20). Moses implored them: "I command you today to love the LORD your God, to walk in obedience to him, and to keep his commands, decrees and laws; then you will live and increase, and the LORD your God will bless you in the land you are entering to possess" (v. 16). On the other hand, their disobedience would result in "death and destruction" (v. 15). Truly, if they disobeyed, they would "not live long in the land you are crossing the Jordan to enter and possess" (v. 18). They would be cast out of it again.[9]

Eden came to be associated as early as the sixth century BCE" (Tuell, "The Rivers of Paradise: Ezekiel 47:1–12 and Genesis 2:10–14," *God Who Creates*, 176.

7. See Tuell, "The Rivers of Paradise," 171–89.

8. Wenham, "Sanctuary Symbolism in the Garden of Eden Story," 401–3.

9. As Wenham notes about the connection between sanctuary and garden: "According to later cultic ritual the sanctuary was the centre of life, because there

The people of Israel were called to right fellowship with God in keeping their sanctuary practices, seeking wisdom, and following God's commandments.[10] Proverbs, like Genesis 2, affirms that wisdom "is a tree of life to those who embrace her" (3:18, NLT). As the Israelites in exile learned, they could not have it both ways; they could not be disobedient and remain in God's blessings. Or, as Genesis puts it, they could not follow in the paths of their own wisdom and "take also from the tree of life and eat, and live forever" (3:22). As they chose to live apart from fellowship with "the living and wise God," they would have to face the increased toil and peril of their alienation from God and life outside the garden.[11] That is the natural consequence of not following the source of their own life and well-being.

At the start of the Genesis 2 narrative, the earth had a problem: there was no vegetation because the earth lacked both rain and human beings "to work the ground" (v. 5). God provided both missing pieces; God watered "the whole surface of the ground" (v. 6), and "the LORD God formed a man from the dust of the ground and breathed into his nostrils the breath of life, and the man became a living being" (v. 7). This statement about humans stands out. First, the human (*adam*) is formed from the dirt (*adamah*). The name "humankind" is a shortened form of "ground," the stuff out of which we come and for which we are created to labor.[12] Second, while humans and animals are equally *living beings*

God was present. To be excluded from the camp of Israel . . . was to enter the realm of death. . . . Thus the expulsion of Adam and Eve from the garden was in the narrator's view the real fulfillment of the divine sentence. He regarded their alienation from the divine presence as death" (404; see Richard J. Clifford, SJ, "Learning from our (first) parents: Can we see Adam and Eve anew?" *America: The Jesuit Review* (October 24, 2014), https://www.americamagazine.org/faith/2014/10/24/learning-our-first-parents-can-we-see-adam-and-eve-anew.

10. Clifford, "Creatio ex nihilo," 68.

11. Clifford, "Creatio ex nihilo," 67.

12. Several languages play with this fundamental connection: *adam* from *adamah* (Hebrew), *human* from *humus* (Latin), *earthling* from the *earth* (English).

and have *the breath of life in their nostrils* (Gen. 7:21-22; see Ps. 104:29-30), humans are the only creature about whom we are given the description of God blowing breath into their nostrils. The awkwardness of sharing breath face to face is a barrier that every CPR class has to confront. Yet God leans into this connection of intimacy and vital dependence.

Genesis 2 does not directly say humans were created in God's image, as reflections of God's own dominion as Redeemer-Creator-Ruler. Even so, human work is meant to serve as part of God's response to the earth's predicament—its uncultivated state. God repeatedly gets dirty hands by working the soil—forming the man from the dust (v. 7), planting a garden (v. 8), making trees grow (v. 9), and forming animals from the ground (v. 19). Our tending of the land participates in God's care for the land. Human work is a priestly mediation of God's blessings, which is even indicated by the priestly verbs that characterize their farming work as "tending and keeping" (*abad* and *shamar*, Gen. 2:15; Num. 3:7-8; 8:26; 18:5-6).

The earth was not created for humankind. Rather, humankind was created from the earth and for the earth. God graciously breathes life into our earthen nostrils so that, as living creatures, we can be agents of life for the earth. The only way for us to do that is to walk obediently in the ways of the Life Giver. God is the only one who possesses life inherently. We, as recipients of divine blessing, are created to bless. We are meant to image God by walking in the flow of God's work on behalf of the earth and its inhabitants. At the same time, humankind—through the rhythms of worship—directs the bounty of creation toward its true purpose and fulfillment in God.

This narrative of life or death goes to the end of Genesis 4. (Genesis 5:1 is where the next story begins—with the next introductory *toledot*.) In Genesis 2-4, we see the life God means for us to live contrasted with humanity's distrust of God's good intentions, humankind walking with God contrasted with humankind hiding from God, and humankind's sweaty work of blessing contrasted with humankind's bloody preoccupation with violence. Yet, even when Adam and Eve did not trust in the Lord's ways and devised their own way, God graciously clothed them as priests (2:21; see Exod. 28:41; 29:8; 40:14; Lev. 8:13) and sent them to work the ground (v. 23).[13] Their sons were still doing priestly work and lifting the bounty of the world to the Lord in worship (4:3–5). Tragically, when humanity's most essential priestly function in the world goes wrong, we get sidetracked and do the opposite of bless. Cain walked the path toward bloodshed. This rejection of priestly vocation quickly escalated to Lamech's decree that he would avenge himself seventy-seven times—eleven times beyond the protections God promised Cain (4:24; see Matt. 18:21–22).

Life or death, blessing or curse—these are the options. God does not intend for the earth to be desolate and barren (Gen. 2:4–7; Isa. 45:18). God is working toward life and lays before creation the way for us all to flourish together. When we distrust God, our resulting disobedience is dis-creative. Our (mal)function leaves a wake of curses and death for all.

Proverbs 8:22–31

The Old Testament has three major sections—Law, Prophets, and Writings.[14] The book of Proverbs is Wisdom Literature, a subsection of the Writings. Proverbs provides

---

13. Wenham, "Sanctuary Symbolism," 401–2. A great resource for understanding the relationship between male and female in Genesis 2–3 is Sarah Derck, "Wynkoop Center Resource: The Creation Mandate," from the Wynkoop Center for Women in Ministry, hosted at the Wesleyan-Holiness Digital Library, http://www.whdl.org/en/browse/resources/9492.

14. The three parts are sometimes named together using the acronym *Tanakh*, which is formed from the beginning sound of the Hebrew name for each part—*Torah* (Law), *Nevi'im* (Prophets), and *Ketuvim* (Writings).

readers with its purpose statement, that it is "for attaining wisdom and discipline" (1:2) and walking rightly with God (v. 7). Like both Genesis 2–4 and Moses's speeches in Deuteronomy, Solomon teaches the young to follow the way of wisdom and not the way of folly. The book's introduction names the two possible paths: "The fear of the Lord is the beginning of knowledge, but fools despise wisdom and instruction" (v. 7). God made the world a certain way, and humankind must learn to live in that created framework—in righteousness (right-ness) and not wickedness.[15] Our righteousness is "not fundamentally a stance of piety but a pattern of behavior which supports rather than subverts the cosmic and moral order."[16]

In Proverbs (especially in the opening section of chapters 1–9), the nature of wisdom is challenging to name. Wisdom is strongly associated with God. A person can fear the Lord or despise wisdom. In a sense, rejecting wisdom is essentially rejecting God. Or positively, to live in reverent obedience to God is to live in wisdom itself. Yet, God is not wisdom, nor is wisdom God. Proverbs uses figurative language about Wisdom and personifies Wisdom several times in the book—for example, 1:20–33; 3:15–18; 8:1–9:12. This personification does not make Wisdom God or a divine agent. She is brought forth "as the first of [God's] works" (8:22). And it is then "by wisdom the Lord laid the earth's foundations, by understanding he set the heavens in place; by his knowledge the watery depths were divided, and the clouds let drop the dew" (3:19–20). Essentially,

---

15. Clifford, "Introduction to Wisdom Literature," *The New Interpreter's Bible*, Vol. 5, 8–9. See also Raymond C. Van Leeuwen, "The Book of Proverbs," *The New Interpreter's Bible*, Vol. 5, 20, 24–25.

16. Douglass Knight, quoted in Sean M. McDonough, *Christ as Creator: Origins of a New Testament Doctrine* (Oxford: Oxford University Press, 2009), 52–53.

what God is doing for the world is wise—or, God's work is done wisely.[17]

Everything God does in creating and acting in the world is in Wisdom. The whole arrangement of creation was mediated through Wisdom; or, as Wisdom says, "I was the artisan at [God's] side" (8:30).[18] Wisdom was delighting God at the same time that Wisdom was delighting in the world (v. 30). This sounds like the Genesis 1 affirmation, "This is good!" Wisdom affirms, "I was pleased with his world and pleased with its people" (v. 31; CEV). Wisdom is not merely an abstract principle or code. It is a manner of functioning. God's presence, coupled with the world's characteristics, epitomizes Wisdom. The crossroad of God's presence and the world functioning as intended is Wisdom's highest joy; it means peace, life, and blessing (3:16–18). Wisdom concludes chapter 8 with the declaration: "Blessed are those who listen to me, watching daily at my doors, waiting at my doorway. For those who find me find life and receive favor from the LORD. But those who fail to find me harm themselves; all who hate me love death" (vv. 34–36). Proceeding according to the wisdom in which we were established means life. Life unfolds in the intersection of God's presence and functioning as we were intended.

Proverbs follows the ancient Near East's understanding of the world's shape by using the structure of the heavens, waters, and land features. Also, like one approach of ancient Near Eastern creation accounts, Proverbs first negates all features—noting a "before," when there were *no* oceans, springs, mountains, hills, earth, fields, or dust (8:23–26). Nevertheless, these stock features of the world's structure

---

17. See Van Leeuwen, "The Book of Proverbs," 96.
18. The 2011 NIV puts "the artisan" in a footnote instead of translating the Hebrew word *amon* ("artisan," "master worker"), as the 1984 NIV did: "I was the craftsman at his side."

and how to narrate creation do not take away from the rich claims being made.

In only three verses, the text moves through God's initial creative work. It names a variety of God's activities: set in place, marked out, established, fixed, and gave boundary (vv. 27–29). Some of the description compares well with Genesis 1. For example, some features of day 2 relate to Proverbs 8:27: God set the heavens by marking "out the horizon on the face of the deep." Clouds were placed above (v. 28). Day 3 compares with the Proverbs statement that God gave the earth foundations and gave a boundary to the sea (v. 29). With so few details, the process of establishing creation does not stand out. The point of emphasis is that God did everything *in wisdom*. God did not stumble into or bumble through creating. Creation is not a necessary outflow from God—in other words, it is not something God could not help *but* do. The first thing from God in relation to the world is wisdom (v. 22). God proceeds wisely and not due to fate, chance, determinism, self-interest, or anything else. God moves toward a Creator-creature relation according to wisdom. Wisdom "was appointed from eternity, from the beginning, before the world began" (v. 23). The outflow of God's wise work evokes delight and rejoicing from Wisdom (vv. 30–31).

With as little as Proverbs says about God's processes of establishing creation, it may seem that Proverbs does not care about creation or have much of a creation theology, but this is not the case. The emphasis is rather on the character of life to be lived between God and creation. God creating in wisdom frames all of life. God's creative activity is not merely a point of information about the past. Wisdom runs through everything, always. From the beginning, the unfolding of wisdom in creation standardizes our "cosmic context" for what we ought to do.[19] This wisdom is good for us even now. It is a good gift from our good Creator. Not only are the features of the world established in wisdom, but wisdom also regulates human society. It marks the edges of the page on which we write our lives.[20]

Psalm 104

Psalm 104 is a creation psalm that delights in God, who reigns and is "clothed with splendor and majesty" (v. 1). God fills the unfolding creation from the start, and from top to bottom (vv. 2–4)—in one regard like filling a garment (v. 2). Through the creative process, God is establishing (vv. 2–3, 5–9) and furnishing a residence (vv. 3–4, 10–15), not only for God but also for every creature (vv. 11–16, 24). God gives each piece a suitable place to reside and time to do its work, sometimes alternating who is active at which time in the same space (vv. 16–23). There is ample fertility and abundance in the world, and everything works together; water refreshes, trees shelter, grass feeds, the sun and moon order time, and so on. Even with the uncountable multitudes of living things, God provides directly for them all (v. 24–27). In addition, the exceeding greatness of God is over all things—from the wildest and mightiest creature (vv. 18, 21, 26) to the largest features of the earth (vv. 7–9, 32). Nothing is exempt. God's care goes down to each individual, and God's rule extends over all.

---

19. Van Leeuwen, "The Book of Proverbs," 26. As Clifford notes, the order of wisdom "was given privileged expression on the day of creation" ("Introduction to Wisdom Literature," 8–9).

20. This is not unlike the way the notion of *torah* overlays Genesis 1. "In Jewish tradition, the move has been to identify Torah (the written and oral law or teaching given to Moses by God at Mt. Sinai) with Wisdom. The correlation of Torah and cosmic wisdom (or Word) is suggested already in several biblical passages (Deut. 4:6–8; Pss. 19:1–10; 33:4–9; 119:89–104; 147:15–20)" (Van Leeuwen, "The Book of Proverbs," 99).

The psalmist begins and ends these celebrations blessing the Lord (vv. 1, 35). Given the sum of the psalm, the writer will overflow in lifelong song to God (v. 33). Yet, even in the psalmist's enthusiasm, the psalmist desires that each meditation would be rightly subject to God (v. 34). This person takes a posture of submission. Even more, in the wonder of all these thoughts, the singer prays that anyone who does not rightly submit to the Lord would "be no more" (v. 35). Wickedness has no appropriate place in the picture. The only place for creation to exist is under God's rule.

One unique feature of this psalm is in verse 31: "May the Lord rejoice in his works." In the Bible, "with the possible exception of Isaiah 9:17, the Hebrew verb *śmḥ* ("be joyful") never takes God as its subject," making this psalm, then, the lone place where "the creator is to rejoice in the creatures."[21] This makes an interesting counterpoint to the multiple references in Scripture to God's covenant love or covenant faithfulness—binding God to creation (see the covenant of Genesis 9). Divine joyfulness even makes an interesting counterpoint to the greatness and majesty of God in this psalm. With all that God provides (drink, shelter, food), every inhabitant is "satisfied with good things" (v. 28). Even beyond a giving and receiving that satisfies, the psalmist's heart overflows toward the Lord and imagines that God might be rejoicing in return. If God made everything "in wisdom" (v. 24), and elsewhere we hear that wisdom playfully delights in the world (Prov. 8:30–31), then the psalmist may be asking of God what God is already doing: going beyond a dutiful role and rejoicing in God's works (v. 31).[22] That may not be much to ask. After all, this is the God who already goes beyond bare necessity in "bringing forth food from the earth: wine that gladdens

---

21. Brown, *The Seven Pillars of Creation*, 147–48.
22. Brown, *The Seven Pillars of Creation*, 149.

human hearts, oil to make their faces shine, and bread that sustains their hearts" (vv. 14–15).

Isaiah 40-55

Chapters 40–55 of Isaiah are often called Second Isaiah. They come from the time of Israel's exile. In the mind of Judah's people, the land had been emptied of its inhabitants. This point of crisis could have brought an end to Israel's faith in God. After the devastation they experienced, they could have thought God was weak or less than divine. They could have thought Babylon's gods ruled everything. Instead, the scriptures from this period in Israel's history have many affirmations about God as unquestionably the Redeemer-Creator-Ruler of the heavens and the earth (e.g., Gen. 1:1–2; Isa. 45:18–19).[23] In fact, in the hardships God's people were facing for their infidelity, they recognized that God "creates" darkness and woe, not some other god (see Isa. 45:6b–7).[24] In this case, there was divine purpose to their experience of devastation. God was working what God intended to work in the world.

These few chapters have one-third of all the Hebrew Bible's uses of the word *bara* ("create").[25] This period sparked an explosion of theological reflection about God's status as Creator. Rather than despairing over the possibility that God is nothing, these chapters comfort Israel with clarifications of God's place as Ruler over them and all creation. "Comfort, comfort my people, says your God. Speak tenderly to Jerusalem, and proclaim to her that her hard service has been completed, that her sin has been paid for, that she has received from the LORD's hand double for

---

23. See Brown, *The Seven Pillars of Creation*, 198–99, 203.
24. Brown, *The Seven Pillars of Creation*, 205.
25. See chapter 3, note 20.

all her sins" (Isa. 40:1–2). Their Redeemer, the Creator of all, would create a new situation for them.

These chapters provide perspective concerning Israel's situation. For example, given that God has weighed all parts of creation and cupped them in God's hands, and given that God can measure the world by just one breadth of God's hand, all people and nations are miniscule, but a vapor to God (Isa. 40:10–17). Nothing on earth is comparable to God; we are not dealing with a deity like those of the nations (vv. 18–20, 23). God can sweep away the mightiest rulers with a small puff. God "sits enthroned above the circle of the earth, and its people are like grasshoppers. He stretches out the heavens like a canopy, and spreads them out like a tent to live in" (v. 22). If God can individually place the innumerable stars and give each one attention, then God surely misses no detail of our own lives (vv. 26–27). God "gives breath to [the earth's] people, and life to those who walk on it" (42:5). God is immense and everlasting, so God will not trail off in holding us up (40:28–31). With every generation from the beginning, it is the Lord "who has done this and carried it through" (41:4).

Israel is about to experience a complete turnaround in their situation. Their God, who can blow away nations and kings (41:2), will gather Israel from the farthest corners (vv. 8–10). Anyone who comes against them "will be as nothing at all" (v. 12). In fact, God's people will be an instrument to thresh even the mountains (vv. 15–16). The text moves between the incomparable capacities of God and the continual faithfulness and fine attention God gives to God's creation. As creatures, we have basic needs and search to meet them; our Creator makes sure needs are met—like providing rivers and pools for the thirsty (vv. 17–20).[26] God holds up our lives.

The text steadily affirms that God is the lone deity. It is God who is "your Redeemer, who formed you in the womb: I am the LORD, the Maker of all things, who stretches out the heavens, who spreads out the earth by myself" (44:24). There is no reason for God to share God's glory or praise for what God has done, or is about to do for exiled Israel (42:8–9; see 48:6–7). It is absurd that any people would ever turn to sorcery (47:9–12) and the reading of signs (vv. 13–15), or shape anything God has made into an idol and turn to it (40:18–20; 44:9–20). God is not something we fashion and cart about (46:1–2, 6–7); rather, God fashions us and sustains us (vv. 3–4). There is a steady beat throughout the text designating God as the one "who created the heavens, he is God; he who fashioned and made the earth, he founded it" (45:18). As a steady counterpoint in the text, idols are nothing. Our only recourse is to the one and only God. "There is no other Rock" (44:8).

God let Israel be carried off (42:14–25; 52:4–6), but just as God once created Israel (43:1, 7) God will make them anew through another act of deliverance (43:1–28; 51:9–16).[27] We can remember back to chapter 3 that *bara* has more to do with working out the function of something than with producing its substance. The concept of *bara* is more like *making a new situation that is to function according to divine purposes.* God's creative work is not relegated to the

---

26. This is quite a contrast from Marduk in Babylon's Enuma Elish. Marduk manipulates the gods to work in his favor and creates humankind as slave laborers to take care of the gods' needs.

27. "As in the psalms, the prophet regards the desperate situation of Israel as an eclipse of creation order. But unlike the psalms that pray the Lord will enact again his creation victory in the future, the prophet has discerned that the Lord is doing that act of creation and exodus at the present time. He therefore urges Israel to take part in the new act, to embark boldly in a new exodus that will display the Lord's glory to the nations" (Clifford, *"Creatio ex nihilo,"* 71).

past; God continues to bring about new situations that God means to function according to God's purposes.

Second Isaiah has many references to God's creative work with the heavens and the earth, but also God *creates* Israel by reestablishing them. The people will come to know God's name (52:6). The LORD is "your Redeemer, the Holy One of Israel . . . your Holy One, Israel's Creator, your King" (43:14–15). Redeemer, Creator, and King belong together as a single constellation for Israel's Holy One (see 44:6, 24; 45:11; 47:4; 54:5). "This is what the LORD says—your Redeemer, the Holy One of Israel: 'I am the LORD your God, who teaches you what is best for you, who directs you in the way you should go. If only you had paid attention to my commands, your peace would have been like a river, your well-being like the waves of the sea'" (48:17–18). As subjects under God's creative activity, humankind does not get to question what the Ruler is making (45:7–12), or God's purposes (46:9–11). Thankfully, God "did not create [the world] to be empty, but formed it to be inhabited" (45:18; see 51:3). God means to rain down righteousness (45:8; 55:8–13), which is necessary to bring about salvation (46:13). "Shower, O heavens, from above, and let the clouds rain down righteousness. Let the earth open so that salvation may spring up, and let it cause righteousness to sprout up also. I YHWH have created it" (45:8).[28] Like rain, God's righteousness, Word, and Spirit accomplish their goals (44:1–4; 55:10–11). God formed Israel once by taking them out of Egypt and journeying with them through the wilderness (43:16–17); God is going to form them again, that they may rightly praise the Holy One (vv. 18–21) and that the land and the people in it would flourish in God's purposes.

The coming restoration will involve all creation: Babylon and its king, the nations, the land, and God's covenant

---

28. Translation by Brown, *The Seven Pillars of Creation*, 207.

people (49:6, 8–9). The earth and its people are each flourishing gardens, sprouting under God's care. They blossom in mutuality between one another.[29] When humankind goes astray, the land becomes desolate. Restoration works in both realms—of the earth and its inhabitants. God means for this renewal to be everlasting (54:9–10; 55:3, 13).

Ecclesiastes

If much of the tone to this point has been a bit idealistic or sweet-sounding, Ecclesiastes offers a healthy dose of realism. Things do not always work out. The promise that, if we live rightly, things will go well sometimes seems broken. Expectations can be dashed. Our work may not yield results. Outcomes are not guaranteed.[30] Ecclesiastes (meaning "one who leads a congregation," or "teacher") captures this sentiment famously: "'Meaningless! Meaningless!' says the Teacher. 'Utterly meaningless! Everything is meaningless'" (1:2). The Hebrew word *hebel*, translated as "meaningless" in verse 2, conveys the idea of absurdity in the sense of being incomprehensible.[31] It is the most-used word in Ecclesiastes. It is jarring to confront the reality that each thing the Scriptures tell us we are to do or pursue can end up being without merit, unreliable, and useless.[32] Our efforts can amount to a vapor or breath.[33] At any moment of following the right course, our labors can come to nothing, and our lives can end in death.

So many other biblical books give the impression that creation is *heading* somewhere. We are part of a story that is moving along. Every part of creation is involved in a group

---

29. Brown, *The Seven Pillars of Creation*, 208–9.
30. W. Sibley Towner, "The Book of Ecclesiastes," *The New Interpreter's Bible*, Vol. 5, 280.
31. Towner, "The Book of Ecclesiastes," 279–80.
32. Towner, "The Book of Ecclesiastes," 279.
33. Towner, "The Book of Ecclesiastes," 279.

project we are all cooperating to accomplish. Ecclesiastes says instead that we are all on a treadmill, toiling to move forward but only covering ground that keeps coming right back around.[34] For example, the sun does the same thing every day (1:5); the water cycle keeps water flowing into the ocean and starting over again, without ever filling it (v. 7); eyes and ears never complete their work (v. 8). Rather than making progress, Ecclesiastes says we go nowhere in our lifetimes. This perspective about life may be due to several features. One is that the author does not talk about a beginning point. The biblical norm is that purpose is tied to beginning. Purpose is conferred at an originating event: "Elsewhere in the Bible, genesis [or beginning] and purpose are inseparably wedded."[35] Without reference to creation, the perspective of Ecclesiastes has no *telos*—only toil.[36] The vantage point is our own human vantage point in the midst of creation's cycles.[37] In many respects, that is the only point of view humans can have. Ecclesiastes offers instruction of what to do in the reality of where we live in our relatively short lives.

As finite creatures, Ecclesiastes counsels the assembly not to live in a way that we are trying to press beyond ourselves. Ecclesiastes does not claim to know too much, to raise so high as to have access into the mind of God. We are also not supposed to overflow our bounds through pursuing fame, money, vast wisdom and knowledge, pleasure, advancement, or great projects. Racing toward greatness is absurd. "All share a common destiny—the righteous and the wicked, the good and the bad, the clean and the unclean, those who offer sacrifices and those who do not. . . . For the living know that they will die" (Eccl. 9:2a, 5a). We

---

34. See Brown, *The Seven Pillars of Creation*, 180.
35. Brown, *The Seven Pillars of Creation*, 181.
36. See Brown, *The Seven Pillars of Creation*, 181.
37. Towner, "The Book of Ecclesiastes," 283.

share a common mortality. We share a common human finitude. Ecclesiastes is not pulling us back to make us fatalistic, asking us to resign ourselves to death. Rather, it grounds us in true wisdom and erases false visions of creaturely purpose and life. As Sibley Towner summarizes the teacher's message: "'All' of human experience is 'absurd'—i.e., incomprehensible, even senseless. Life is 'toil.' With the help of 'wisdom' a person may find happiness amid the toil, but only if that person is utterly realistic about the inevitable 'fate' of death."[38] There is no value in the pursuit of surpassing our finitude. Instead, we are meant to deeply inhabit our life in the world. We are earthlings (*adam*) of the earth (*adamah*).

> Go, eat your food with gladness, and drink your wine with a joyful heart, for God has already approved what you do. Always be clothed in white, and always anoint your head with oil. Enjoy life with your wife, whom you love, all the days of this meaningless life that God has given you under the sun—all your meaningless days. For this is your lot in life and in your toilsome labor under the sun. Whatever your hand finds to do, do it with all your might, for in the realm of the dead, where you are going, there is neither working nor planning nor knowledge nor wisdom. (Eccl. 9:7–10)

God has disclosed a righteous and wise way to live in the time we are given. We are to savor and enjoy life, to dig our toes into the soil. "God wills that we love life."[39]

This is not a book about a collective human endeavor, whether in the positive sense of making the world fulfill God's purposes or in the negative sense of building a tower of Babel. It is not our place to be bigger than a finite human being and pile up experiences, resources, or fame for

---

38. Towner, "The Book of Ecclesiastes," 282.
39. Towner, "The Book of Ecclesiastes," 357.

ourselves. Certainly, it is great to know, like many creation texts show, what story we are living and that God has purposes for creation. It is great to live faithfully in the wisdom God has given us to live. We must recognize, however, that we may never get anywhere or reap rewards for doing it. We can savor what comes in the moment of doing what is wise, but it is absurd to do it for greatness, or because we have certainty about receiving a reward.

Job 38–41

If any humans are ever tempted to think the world is all about them and for their purposes, the book of Job will quickly correct them. The wisdom and justice God is working in the world are beyond us.[40] It surpasses our knowledge and authority to challenge them. As God asks Job: ""Who is this that obscures my plans with words without knowledge?" (38:2) and "Will the one who contends with the Almighty correct him?" (40:2). We are a small piece in something so much grander than us and the part we are given to play.

Humans have a variety of ideas about God and responses to the world.[41] Job was tempted to think God was acting in the world and in his situation randomly and unjustly (12:25). Yet the LORD asked him, "Would you discredit my justice? Would you condemn me to justify yourself?" (40:8; see 42:3). Job's friends looked at the world and only saw order, God's majesty, or the need to marvel at God. They had not read Ecclesiastes, so they thought everything always worked according to a system of receiving blessings and curses in accordance with what we have done. Yet, as the book of Job notes, the LORD makes terrifying beasts that humans cannot stop, and God intends for the beasts

---

40. Clifford, "*Creatio ex nihilo,*" 74.
41. See Clifford, "*Creatio ex nihilo,*" 73.

to be as much a part of creation as humankind (40:15; 41:1, 25–29). God's world has wild characters and dangerous characteristics within it. They do not function unchecked; even so, they are still there. This is not due to the world being fallen; it is by God's design. Certainly human sin destroys and dis-creates in ways God never intended. Nevertheless, there are terrifying dimensions to the way creation operates that God intended and built into creation's shared life. These wild things, that often inhabit barren and empty places, operate within the tidy cosmic structures we may overemphasize. They are subject to God and God's care.

Humans are limited in our perspective. God was at work long before we arrived, and we cannot delve into every nook and cranny of creation to know what God has done or is doing there (Job 38). We may see senselessness in different parts of the world or its creatures. Ostrich wings do not work like those of storks, and they lay their eggs on the ground, but they sure can run (39:13–18). Horses, hawks, and eagles also all have their unique characteristics (39:19–30). God has done all of these things in wisdom yet does not explain to Job what that wisdom is. God alone has the capacity to be God and to rule all things as Creator, according to wisdom and justice: "everything under heaven belongs to me" (41:11). Even the fiercest beasts that wreak havoc in the world, God holds on a leash.

When the Lord has finished teaching Job, Job acknowledges God's points and repents (42:1–6). This book started with a question about whether Job was truly righteous. Through all his suffering and loss, he never sinned. It ends with Job speaking truth about God and being able to intercede for others in prayer (42:8). In the resolution, God clearly shows that God is capable of acting justly and does act justly. Thus, as much as God speaks to Job about the cosmos and the many creatures God has created in chapters

38–41, "God also prizes and honors Job, and finally restores what he has lost."[42]

Conclusion

These texts offer vitally important perspectives. If we only had Genesis 1, we might become horribly overconfident about our place in the world. After hearing that we are created to image God in the world, humankind might go out and live as though the reigns are in our hands—like we were a sub-deity over the world. These other texts continue to affirm who sits on the throne and what our place is as God's subjects. We are not to imagine we control the course of history or the world's destiny. We are not to imagine we are even lords of our own lives, trying to rise above our limited station and live according to our own wisdom. We are not meant to play God's part. God has revealed the big picture of God's intent for creation. But we are not to take over God's role in legislating and governing. We have finite lifetimes and finite reach. Our burden is to live faithfully in God's wisdom, where we are planted, in the time we have.

From the beginning, God has acted as Creator in wisdom. We do not have the full scope of what that is, and life may seem chaotic and arbitrary from where we stand. It may be tempting to sit passively as though some divinely worked-out fate is coming our way. However, every passage explored here calls us to conduct ourselves in the paths of wisdom. Wisdom is not a deterministic roadmap. Rather, it illuminates the ground ahead of us so that we, in our own agency, can walk without stumbling. These passages do not suggest that God leaves us alone or is too lofty to be concerned with our issues. God knows our business and is attentive to each part of the world. God means to walk together with us as God inhabits God's creation.

---

42. Clifford, "*Creatio ex nihilo*," 74.

Creation in the New Testament

six

Christians should not be surprised that many of the Old Testament perspectives about God as Creator of all things carry forward into the New Testament. It would actually be disturbing if God all of a sudden became a different God.¹ The New Testament clarifies how Jesus, the Messiah, fits into the framework of Israel's God, who is Redeemer, Creator, and Ruler of all things (see Isa. 43:14–15; 44:6, 24; 45:11; 47:4; 54:5).² The Old Testament had already connected the themes of salvation and creation as part of the same dynamic; salvation is a new act of creation.³ Even further, as God's *people* experienced restoration through creation, *all nature* also experienced restoration. This same

---

1. One of the earliest heresies in Christianity is Marcionism—named after its founder, Marcion (c. AD 85–160). He suggested there actually is a difference between divine beings in the Testaments—that Jesus in the New Testament is unrelated to the God of the Old Testament.

2. The order of these three titles is intentional for three reasons. First, this is their order in Isaiah. Second, this is the order in which Israel came to experience and understand God—first through acts of salvation and later in reflecting about God as Creator. Third, Paul T. Nimmo makes a point worth considering, given that Christ is truly the center of all reflections about God: "Rather than declaring that it is the work of the incarnation that is 'fitting' for God the Creator, it might be more appropriate to declare that it is the work of creation and providence that is 'fitting' for God the Reconciler. In other words, God's wisdom in creation and providence is oriented to and circumscribed by the divinely enacted event of reconciliation, rather than the other way around. The order of nature is indeed ministerial to the order of grace" (Nimmo, "The Divine Wisdom and the Divine Economy," *Modern Theology* 34:3 [2018]: 414).

3. McDonough, *Christ as Creator*, 49, 63.

theology carries through the New Testament.[4] God is saving the world through Christ, by the Holy Spirit, through creative activity (a new creation or re-creation). According to the teaching of the New Testament, this redeeming, creative, sovereign action of God, through the Son, by the Holy Spirit, is not new to God. There is no time when God has ever been or ever will be different from this triune nature. Even if it only became evident in Christ, that does not mean God has not always been triune.

The logic of the New Testament is delightful in the way all three divine roles of Redeemer, Creator, and Ruler come together for the Father, Son, and Holy Spirit. First, in the ancient world, the one who creates is unquestionably God. Creator is the highest office because that being institutes the arrangement of all other things and their operations. The Creator is the one in command, with every other person, place, and thing a subject under the Creator's rule. Creating what ought to be the case within creation (legislating, governing) is something only the Creator-Ruler has authority to do. Not only does God hold the office with surpassing majesty, but God is also incomparably vast to the combined scale of all other things. There is Creator (God), and everything else. In the early church, one of the clearest and highest claims a theologian could make about the Son or Spirit being equally divine with the Father was to call them Cre-

---

4. Christoph Stenschke, "Human and Non-Human Creation and Its Redemption in Paul's Letter to the Romans," *Neotestamentica* 51.2 (2017): 262–63, 274. Stenschke asserts that Romans 8 carries forward the creation theme from Romans 1 (265). See Howard Snyder and Joel Scandrett, *Salvation Means Creation Healed* (Eugene, OR: Cascade Books, 2011). Furthermore, just as God's Spirit is linked to the creation and renewal of the world in Old Testament and early Jewish sources, human life will be renewed by the same Spirit (Stenschke, 267–68; Stenschke recommends seeing Isa. 32:1–8; 43:16; 44:1–5; Ps. 104:29f.; and Ezek. 36–37). John's Gospel also connects creation themes with God's saving work. See Jeannine K. Brown, "Creation's Renewal in the Gospel of John," *The Catholic Biblical Quarterly* 72 (2010): 275–90; Vail, *Atonement and Salvation*, 63–74; Vail, *Eschatology*, 45–49.

ator—placing them on that throne, in that office.[5] The Son and Spirit do not answer to a higher being; they *are* that very being, as one God: Father, Son, and Holy Spirit.[6]

Second, redemption requires an act of creation.[7] For example, if the present arrangement of nations has one group subject to another group, the Creator-Ruler can declare a new arrangement. If Israel was suffering under other nations, God could re-create the situation. God could establish their new place in the world, raising them up as a beacon or disciplinarian against unjust nations. In turn, if Israel was unfaithful, God could once again re-create Israel's place and function in order to correct them.

Third, redemption must ultimately come from God, to whom all things are subject. God's goodness, sovereignty, and power are all at play here. If the world works in directions outside of God's purposes for it, those works will not stand in the end. Creation will come to function according to God's purposes in the glory of God. It must be emphasized that the goodness of God is just as much the issue here as God's sovereignty. God, in all God's love,

---

5. "It is precisely the truth that Jesus Christ is creator and ruler of all things that undergirds the Christian confession that Jesus is God." (Simon Gathercole, "Pre-existence, and the Freedom of the Son in Creation and Redemption: An Exposition in Dialogue with Robert Jenson," *International Journal of Systematic Theology* 7:1 (2005): 47). Saying the earth and all creation are the works of the Father, Son, and Holy Spirit is to place them equally and fully as God. The fourth-century orthodox theologians consistently showed from Scripture that the Son and Spirit were creator and, therefore, God.

6. Christ's earliest converts had an "unwavering commitment to a monotheistic faith. It is therefore no coincidence that Christ is never depicted in the New Testament as a 'second god.' . . . There is one God, and Jesus as his agent is enfolded within the divine identity. He is depicted neither as a rival for God's throne, nor a semidivine subordinate" (McDonough, *Christ as Creator*, 134).

7. Remember from chapters 3 and 4 that for God to create (*bara*) is to bring about new situations that were not there before God's action. In the Old Testament, *bara* does not name the materials out of which things come to be. Rather, an act of creation establishes a new set of circumstances and how things are to function in it.

will not let the world end in destruction. While individuals and groups try to rewrite the ways God intends the world to function, only God can oversee the flourishing of all things in the fullness of God's wisdom.[8] True salvation (*shalom* for all creation) can only be established in God's great wisdom because only in the wisdom of God can all things be re-created into a way of living so that every facet of the heavens and earth thrives in the glory of God's love. Only the Creator has the capacity to write a true, good, and beautiful redemption story for all creation—from the smallest to the mightiest. God's redemption re-creates all things to flourish in the triune love of God. This happens in Christ, by the Holy Spirit.

God with Us

At Jesus's birth, God's angel declared the good news to the shepherds that, "Today in the town of David a Savior has been born to you; he is the Messiah, the Lord" (Luke 2:11). It is a profound confession to say, "that this man really is the Savior of the world" (John 4:42). If Jesus is the Savior of the world, if saving requires a divine act of re-creation, and if Israel's Holy One alone is Creator (God), then Jesus *must* be Immanuel—God with us. Furthermore, if the Messiah is God with us (doing this redeeming-creating work that God alone can do), then this same Messiah (the Spirit-bearer) must always have had this status with God, being Creator-Ruler.[9] God creates and saves through the Son, by the Spirit. The New Testament declares Christ's divinity as Redeemer-Creator-Ruler; he is not one of God's

---

8. Nimmo, "The Divine Wisdom," 409; see also Christopher A. Beetham, "From Creation to New Creation," *From Creation to New Creation: Biblical Theology and Exegesis, Essays in Honor of G. K. Beale*, Daniel M. Gurtner and Benjamin L. Gladd, eds. (Peabody, MA: Hendrickson Publishers, 2013), 237.

9. See McDonough, *Christ as Creator*, 43, 46.

creations.¹⁰ If he were lesser than fully God (with all wisdom, authority, power, and love), he could not rightly or adequately execute the office of Redeemer-Creator-Ruler. As God, however, Christ does the work and is worthy of the same praises as God (compare Rev. 5:12 and 7:12).

It is not that Jesus's disciples wanted Jesus to be divine and made up Jesus's divinity. They were *witnesses* of his amazing deeds and Jesus's "remarkable power over the created order," all of which served "to restore the creation to its intended role as a source of blessing."¹¹ This Spirit-bearing Messiah could calm seas and walk on water. He could provide wine at a wedding feast and food for the multitudes. Fish swarmed into nets that he ordered to be cast. He raised the dead, healed the sick, and delivered the possessed. Indeed, the way Jesus healed the man who was born blind—by making mud and putting it on his eyes (John 9:6–7)—sparks the memory of God forming Adam from the ground (Gen. 2:7).

Even Jesus's teaching was not like those who merely explained God's law; "he taught as one who had authority" (Matt. 7:29; see Matt. 28:18 and Mark 1:27). People marveled at the wisdom and power he possessed (Matt. 13:54; Mark 6:2; see 1 Cor. 1:24). As Paul explained, in him "all the fullness of the Deity lives in bodily form" (Col. 2:9; see v. 3).¹² His authority extended to the forgiveness of sins

---

10. See McDonough, *Christ as Creator*, 2–3, 67–69. It is important to avoid heresies that do not accept Christ's divine nature. One of them is called adoptionism (or dynamic monarchianism). In this view, God adopts the human Jesus into divine status. Another heresy is Arianism, named after Arius from the third and fourth centuries, who taught that the Father *made* the Son as the first creation. The Son, being created divine, was able to carry out God's will in creating everything else and becoming incarnate to save everything. Both adoptionism and Arianism were condemned as heresies at the first Christian council in 325, held in Nicaea.

11. McDonough, *Christ as Creator*, 22.

12. It is important to clarify that Christianity does not teach that *God the Father* became incarnate. The three divine Persons—Father, Son, and Holy

(Matt. 9:6) and casting out demons (Mark 1:27). Christ claimed to be in the position of Redeemer-Creator-Ruler, having "all authority in heaven and on earth" (Matt. 28:18).

As the one with the highest cosmic authority, Christ in turn promised to give his disciples "words and wisdom that none of your adversaries will be able to resist or contradict" (Luke 21:15).[13] He conferred authority on his disciples to be agents of redemption (Matt. 10:1); he commanded them to go to all nations (28:19). Parallel to the teachers of the Law, they were to be teachers of his commands—his clarifications of God's purposes for them (28:20). John's Gospel has a similar theology: "The followers of Jesus are those who see that his words are indeed the words of God, just as his deeds are the deeds of God: 'The word which you have heard is not mine, but that of the Father who sent me' (14:24)."[14] Christ is "the image of the invisible God" (Col. 1:15) and "the radiance of God's glory and the exact representation of his being, sustaining all things by his powerful word" (Heb. 1:3). God's wisdom is given by Christ, as well as by the Spirit (1 Cor. 2:13; Eph. 1:17; Col. 1:9). Paul and the apostles admonished and taught in that wisdom (Col. 1:28; 3:16; 2 Pet. 3:15; see Luke 1:17), and believers were to grow and live in it (James 1:5; 3:13, 17). The disciples experienced God's redemptive-creative work through Christ and then became agents of that work. God's sovereign purposes in creation get worked out in and through Christ, by the

---

Spirit—are distinguished from one another, even while we do not say that God gets divided up between the three, or that we have three gods. For all eternity, God is all three Persons. One of the heresies in Christianity is modalism, which teaches that God is not really triune and that God the Father becomes incarnate as the Son and then comes as the Spirit. We should not read Colossians 2:9 like modalism does when Paul says, "For in Christ all the fullness of the Deity lives in bodily form." Instead, the Son is fully divine, just as Father and Spirit are fully divine, even while it is only the Son who took on flesh.

13. See Nimmo, "The Divine Wisdom," 412.

14. McDonough, *Christ as Creator*, 218–19; see Nimmo, "The Divine Wisdom," 404.

Spirit. Whatever sinful distortions have come into humankind and the world, in Christ God is recreating everything in the love of God.

No doubt, God was founding a new covenant in Christ, but we have to be careful in thinking that God was doing something *entirely novel* through Jesus the Messiah.[15] From the Old to New Testament, there is continuity in who God is and what God is working toward. "There is an unbroken stream from primal creation, through the ongoing maintenance of creation, and on to eschatological re-creation."[16] What God revealed in Christ may have been hidden until that point, but it does not mean God changed character or had new intentions for creation. God has had an "eternal purpose" that God "accomplished in Christ Jesus our Lord" (Eph. 3:11; see 1 Cor. 2:7). It was actually in God's wisdom and understanding that God's purpose would "be put into effect when the times reach their fulfillment" (Eph. 1:10). From eternity, God "purposed in Christ . . . to bring unity to all things in heaven and on earth under Christ" (vv. 9–10). In him "are hidden all the treasures of wisdom and knowledge" (Col. 2:3).

The New Testament teaches that God has been engaging in redeeming-creating-ruling through the Messiah at all times. "The world is created *within the sphere of his messianic authority*. . . . Christ can rightly be seen from one perspective as the beginning point and the end point of creation, even if the ultimate origin and destiny of all things is God the Father."[17] A breakdown of 1 Corinthians 8:6 in the NASB helps show this relationship:

---

15. See Nimmo, "The Divine Wisdom," 415.
16. McDonough, *Christ as Creator*, 225.
17. McDonough, *Christ as Creator*, 186.

> yet for us there is but
>> one God, the Father,
>>> **from whom** are *all things*
>> and
>>> we exist **for Him**;
> and
>> one Lord, Jesus Christ,
>>> **by whom** are *all things*,
>> and
>>> we exist **through Him**.

While all things are *from* and *for* the Father, there is no separating that from the reality that it is *by* Christ that we are from God and *through* Christ that we exist for God. It is one inseparable movement of God.[18] There is one God—Father, Son, and Holy Spirit—acting inseparably as Father, Son, and Holy Spirit in whom "we live and move and have our being" (Acts 17:28; see Rom. 11:36). Our existence and living and purpose are not from or unto a set of principles or rules that God declares over the world. God gives God's very self for our existence and life, for the purpose of both receiving and giving expression out of God's own love as Father, Son, and Holy Spirit. God's wisdom is functioning in the world because *God* is personally present and active in the world. "Jesus is the effulgence of the Father's majesty . . . the vehicle through which God shares himself with the world."[19] Jesus does not just teach truth and grant life from afar; he is "the way and the truth and the life," and "no one comes to the Father except through" him (John 14:6). Furthermore, "the

---

18. See Gathercole, "Pre-existence and Freedom," 48–49; McDonough, *Christ as Creator*, 155, 168–69.

19. McDonough, *Christ as Creator*, 222. This should be a caution to anyone who wants to argue that Christianity thinks of Christ the *Logos* (Word) in ways that parallel Stoic *logos* (see Nimmo, "The Divine Wisdom and the Divine Economy," 414). This is disqualified in Job 28:12–29 (Nimmo, 414). Wisdom is not in the things of the world, nor can it be bought as though it is itself a thing (Job 28:12–19). Rather, "the fear of the Lord—that is wisdom" (v. 28).

Spirit of truth" also lives in us (v. 17) to teach and prompt us (v. 26; see Acts 8:15–17, 29; 9:31). As much as we are meant to walk in the wisdom and ways of the Lord, we can do that because we are meant to walk in the Lord (John 14:9–26). God gathers us into God's triune life.

The heavens and earth were created to be God's sanctuary. Humankind was meant to tend and keep it as part of our priestly vocation. God is bringing that objective to completion in Christ as all things are brought into unity in Christ (Eph. 1:10). In the book of Revelation, the seer was told about what this will mean in the end: "Look! God's dwelling place is now among the people, and he will dwell with them. They will be his people, and God himself will be with them and be their God" (21:3). At the same time as God abides in our midst, we in turn are gathered into the glory of the Father, Son, and Holy Spirit. So often things are woven both ways in Scripture—God in and with us, us in and with God.

God does a profound creative (re-creative) act of salvation in Christ in order to bring creation to its intended purpose. In, through, and for the Son all things were created, and through him all things are reconciled to God (Col. 1:16, 20). He is above and before all things in both God's creative and re-creative work—"the firstborn over all creation" and "the firstborn from among the dead" (vv. 15, 18). In every action of redemption-creation-ruling, the Son is before all things; he is the beginning—being the head and having supremacy (v. 18). He is Creator-Ruler over "things in heaven and on earth, visible and invisible, whether thrones or powers or rulers or authorities" (v. 16). Nothing can have the universal dominion he has.

God creates through the one and only Son who came in the flesh as Messiah.[20] The Son "shares the divine identity,"

---

20. McDonough, *Christ as Creator*, 71.

and has always mediated God's presence to the world, holding all things together according to God's wisdom.[21] The world is created to operate within or according to messianic authority (see Heb. 1:1–3, 8–13).[22] It is common among biblical scholars to talk about Christ as filling the role wisdom holds in the Old Testament. There may be New Testament passages in which that happens, but in the Gospels, people marveled at his wisdom, authority, and power. In Colossians 2:3, "Christ is the one 'in whom all the treasures of wisdom and knowledge are hidden'. Wisdom, once again, is *in* the Messiah, which is not the same thing as saying Wisdom *is* the Messiah."[23] The Messiah is clearly more than God's agent (a created being) when the New Testament takes Old Testament statements about God as Creator (like Ps. 102:25–27) and attributes them to Christ (Heb. 1:10–12). The Son acts freely as God-with-us and is not simply the highest among God's subjects.[24] The Messiah is in the role of Redeemer-Creator-Ruler, even while we must note God's triune nature as Redeemer-Creator-Ruler—operating from the Father, in and through the Son, by the Spirit.

Creative Acts of Salvation

There is not space here to unpack entirely the ways in which our Redeemer-Creator-Ruler is recreating all things through Christ by the Holy Spirit. There are other books

---

21. McDonough, *Christ as Creator*, 72, 119, 169; see Col. 1:17; 2:2–3, 9.
22. McDonough, *Christ as Creator*, 186, 187.
23. McDonough, *Christ as Creator*, 175–76; see 196–99. We have to be careful not to make the Son a lesser being than what the Scriptures teach. "Messiah" is not an equivalent term to the personification of "Wisdom" in Proverbs 8 (176, 178).
24. As Gathercole writes: "just as the freedom of the Son in the incarnation is required to safeguard against a Son who simply finds himself in the world, so also the freedom of the Son is required in creation. The action of the Son in his redemptive work on the cross is free. If so, it must be that not only his advent, but also his participation in the act of creation—because it entails redemption—must be free" ("Pre-existence and Freedom," 50).

dedicated to God's saving work in Christ, both through his first and second comings.[25] Here is just a taste of salvation by means of creation in Christ.

First, humankind is re-created in God's love because our Creator entered into our humanity. We abandoned our God-given function of imaging God in the world by doing what was right in our own eyes, following our own wisdom. We corrupted ourselves, every societal relationship, all dimensions of our work, and so on, which led to suffering and death for humankind, the earth, and all its inhabitants. The Son of God entered into the line of humanity by taking up human flesh in Mary's womb. Christ is the Second Adam in the story of humanity, rewriting humankind according to God's purposes for us.[26]

Second, Jesus re-created individual life narratives. In the Gospel of Luke, he read Isaiah 61:1–2 in his hometown synagogue: "The Spirit of the Lord is on me, because he has anointed me to proclaim good news to the poor. He has sent me to proclaim freedom for the prisoners and recovery of sight for the blind, to set the oppressed free, to proclaim the year of the Lord's favor" (Luke 4:18–19). Through Jesus's ministry, God was recreating people's situations according to God's intentions—for them to flourish within God's reign or kingdom. He healed sick people and raised the dead. He delivered people from their oppressions: "if I drive out demons by the finger of God, then the kingdom of God has come upon you" (Luke 11:20). The poor in spirit, those who mourn, the meek, those who hunger and thirst for

---

25. For a deeper look at God's saving work through the Son's incarnation, ministry, crucifixion, descent into death, resurrection, ascension, and return, see Vail, *Atonement and Salvation*. For a deeper look at God's ultimate re-creative work at Christ's return to bring the heavens and the earth into the fullness of God's purposes for them, see Vail, *Eschatology*.

26. See Vail, *Atonement and Salvation*, 18–19, 51–62. The transformation of humankind through the divine Word coming into our full humanity is called *recapitulation*.

righteousness, the merciful, the pure in heart, the peacemakers, and the persecuted were no longer overlooked, disenchanted, or crushed; they were at the center of God's care in God's in-breaking rule (Matt. 5:3–12).

Third, Jesus re-created social expectations and norms—including the ones where people had religious reasons for the status quo. Sinners, women, tax collectors, children, and gentiles could be Jesus's disciples, and even models of how to live according to God's purposes. In contrast, the light of God's kingdom exposed darkness in the people who were valued and respected according to cultural norms and human wisdom. These people included men, religious leaders, descendants of Abraham, and people who were wealthy, educated, healthy, or powerful.

Here are several examples. A supposed *righteous man* did nothing to be hospitable to Jesus, but a supposed *sinful woman* cared for Jesus with kisses of welcome, washing his feet and anointing him with perfume (Luke 7:36–50). A rich ruler (assumed to be favored by God) kept the standard list of God's commandments but would not give his possessions to the poor; on the other hand, a rich tax collector (assumed to be a sell-out) was giving half his possessions to the poor and, out of the remaining amount, making amends with anyone he wronged (Luke 18:18–29; 19:1–10). In a similar act of unchecked generosity, a boy gave his entire lunch to feed a multitude (John 6:9). Mary sat at Jesus's feet, like any male trainee would have done, and was praised for it (Luke 10:38–42). The Samaritans celebrated Jesus while the chief priests clung to Caesar (John 4:42; 19:15). A centurion had more faith in Jesus's authority than anyone in Israel (Luke 7:1–10). A man born blind could see who Jesus is better than those who were born with their sight, and he became a sheep of the Good Shepherd while those assumed to be righteous were outsiders (John 9:1–10:21).

God's intention for creation was to inhabit it as God's sanctuary; for eternity, God intended to come in Christ Jesus.

Paul wrote to various churches teaching them the ways Christ re-creates social structures of the world that are built on human wisdom. Social markers that divide and rank people get eliminated by Christ in favor of a side-by-side humanity where everyone together images God in their royal, priestly work. As Paul wrote, "There is neither Jew nor Gentile, neither slave nor free, nor is there male and female, for you are all one in Christ Jesus" (Gal. 3:28). He wrote even further in Ephesians 2 on the issue of a new, unified humanity being created in Christ:

> For we are God's handiwork, created in Christ Jesus to do good works, which God prepared in advance for us to do.
>
> Therefore, remember that formerly you who are Gentiles by birth and called "uncircumcised" by those who call themselves "the circumcision" (which is done in the body by human hands)—remember that at that time you were separate from Christ, excluded from citizenship in Israel and foreigners to the covenants of the promise, without hope and without God in the world. But now in Christ Jesus you who once were far away have been brought near by the blood of Christ.
>
> For he himself is our peace, who has made the two groups one and has destroyed the barrier, the dividing wall of hostility, by setting aside in his flesh the law with its commands and regulations. His purpose was to create in himself one new humanity out of the two, thus making peace, and in one body to reconcile both of them to God through the cross, by which he put to death their hostility. He came and preached peace to you who were far away and peace to those who were near. For through him we both have access to the Father by one Spirit.
>
> Consequently, you are no longer foreigners and strangers, but fellow citizens with God's people and

also members of his household, built on the foundation of the apostles and prophets, with Christ Jesus himself as the chief cornerstone. In him the whole building is joined together and rises to become a holy temple in the Lord. And in him you too are being built together to become a dwelling in which God lives by his Spirit.

(Eph. 2:10–22)

This passage points toward the fourth act of creation. Through the cross and by the Holy Spirit, God took down old barriers, made peace amid hostility, and disarmed all alternate powers, rulers, and authorities. The old ways of sin and death met their end, and God created new ways in their place. Human wisdom sees God's wisdom as foolishness (1 Cor. 1:18–31). Even more, "The mind governed by the flesh is hostile to God; it does not submit to God's law, nor can it do so" (Rom. 8:7; John 3:3). Thus God breaks through our animosity through the cross and remakes us through the resurrection, in the power of the Spirit (Rom. 5:10; see John 3:1–21; 2 Cor. 5:14–20; Col. 2:11–14; 1 Pet. 3:18). Christ put an end to humanity's waywardness and guilt at the cross; we were dead in our sins and the way we were living against God and God's ways (Col. 2:13).[27] At the cross he put an end to what was killing us: "He forgave us all our sins, having canceled the charge of our legal indebtedness, which stood against us and condemned us; he

---

27. As Nimmo writes, "The victory of divine wisdom is the victory not of a disembodied and impersonal divine principle but of an incarnate and personal divine agent—Jesus Christ (1 Thess. 5:9–10). . . . The 'new creation' (2 Cor. 5:17) that is the result of the divine irruption into history in Jesus Christ is the new creation of God who recognizes, receives, and embraces the divine wisdom as true human wisdom, and is able even to enact it. The practical consequences of this salvific wisdom of God are given material contour and color in the repeated references in the Gospel to the recalibration of human attitudes and expectations—in terms of measuring success, of ordering society, of serving faithfully, and of conceiving God" (Nimmo, "The Divine Wisdom," 413).

has taken it away, nailing it to the cross" (Col. 2:13b–14).[28] Our old life (and any guilt that came with it) dies with Christ when we are united with him in his death through baptism, so that we can be "brought to fullness" by being "raised with him" (vv. 10, 12; see Rom. 6).[29] "Therefore, if anyone is in Christ, the new creation has come: The old has gone, the new is here!" (2 Cor. 5:17). His death is the final period at the end of the former story of sin.

Not only does the cross put a stop to the course of human sin and death in the world, but it also puts a stop to the wrong direction of all other powers. As Creator-Ruler, every throne, power, ruler, and authority was created through and for Christ (Col. 1:16); he is head over them all (2:10). The rebellion of the world was on full display when it put the Son to death (Matt. 21:33–39; John 1:9–11). However, "having disarmed the powers and authorities, he made a public spectacle of them, triumphing over them by the cross" (Col. 2:15). God put an end to the tyranny of sin and death in humankind, and God put an end to the tyranny of all powers and principalities at work in the world.[30] The end cleared the ground for a beginning—the

---

28. Robert G. Hall says the book of Hebrews "sees Jesus uniting with everyone facing death in anguish (Heb. 2:9–11, 14–18; 4:15; 12:1–4)." Hall, "Pre-existence, Naming, and Investiture in the Similitudes of Enoch and in Hebrews," *Religion & Theology* 18 (2011): 329. In line with Psalm 102, Jesus calls "to the one who is able to save him (Heb. 5:7) and his followers (Heb. 2:14–15) from death. . . . More precisely, Jesus sings affliction, trust, and petition, and then God sings in answer" (Hall, 329). In other words, death seems like it would be a complete end. However, the groaning gives way to worship (Ps. 102:19–22), and perishing gives way to life in the Lord (vv. 23–28). Jesus unites with us, working on our behalf to take us into that fuller life God is creating. Nimmo writes, "Each foretelling of the cross . . . also prophetically announces the resurrection. And it is a failure to understand that the *telos* of the crucifixion lies in the resurrection that leads to Jesus sharply rebuking the disciples on the road to Emmaus—'Oh, how foolish you are [. . .]!' (Luke 24:25)" (Nimmo, "The Divine Wisdom," 412).

29. See the significance of baptism in Vail, *Atonement and Salvation*, 74–76, 102–4.

30. See Vail, "The New Exodus," *Atonement and Salvation*, 63–76.

creative act. On the first day of the week, the first day of (new) creation, the Son rose from the grave in the power of the Spirit and breathed on the disciples so that they would receive the Holy Spirit and also live in the new creation life (John 20:1, 22).

All of this creative work in Christ was not just a rescue operation because things had gone wrong. God's intention for creation was to inhabit it as God's sanctuary; for eternity, God intended to come in Christ Jesus. Christ was the full revealing of what had been hidden to that point. Christ was the full realization of God's creative purposes. Coming in Christ not only redeemed what had been distorted, but it also so in-filled creaturely existence with God's own divine life that creation could have everlasting life. It re-created our creaturely existence so death could be defeated and one day destroyed. God entered creaturely existence to bless it with the fullness of divine fellowship, and God entered death to change it. Because of the transforming presence of God entering death itself, Paul could declare, "I am convinced that neither death nor life, neither angels nor demons, neither the present nor the future, nor any powers, neither height nor depth, nor anything else in all creation, will be able to separate us from the love of God that is in Christ Jesus our Lord" (Rom. 8:38–39). When Christ returns, death will have to give up its captives, and death will then be no more: "When the perishable has been clothed with the imperishable, and the mortal with immortality, then the saying that is written will come true: 'Death has been swallowed up in victory'" (1 Cor. 15:54). The new, saving acts of God through Christ will be complete at the second coming of Christ.

Paradox

Israel had the most to say about God as Creator during their exile. These affirmations were most important to them in the midst of their collapse and suffering; they declared that God was Lord of all, including over their captors. Jesus's disciples also experienced the crushing blow of their teacher and hoped-for Messiah being betrayed, captured, and crucified. They also experienced persecution and hardships later on. Yet they were certain of who he was, is, and forever will be. Devastation is not always what it seems to be. God remade Israel in her exile. After all she had done, God cleansed her and made her righteous. Exile chopped her down close to the ground, but God faithfully remade the remnant to function according to the fullness of life.

In previous experiences of redemption, God's creation experienced pains on the way. When humankind degraded both itself and the earth with violence (Gen. 6), God used the flood to scrub the earth clean of all but a small remnant (Gen. 7). God then re-created the earth in the same sequence as God had made it before (compare Gen. 8 with Gen. 1). When Israel degraded itself and its land, God scrubbed them from the land through exile before renewing the land and its inhabitants.[31] In Christ, God was willing to shoulder all sin in order to purge it from creation, carrying it into the destruction of death and the grave for our sake (Matt. 18:27; Gal. 3:13; Col. 2:14).[32] "God did not send his Son into the world to condemn the world, but to save the world through him" (John 3:17). It was not just a remnant that would enjoy this redemption, at the loss of so many wicked people and so much hardship endured by the corrupted land. God was not willing to lose *any* (Matt. 18:14); God so loves the world that he gave the Son.

Having united in solidarity with all the corruptions and sufferings of creation, Christ entered the abyss of

---

31. See how destruction functions in Scripture in Vail, *Eschatology*, 71–75.
32. See the function of Christ as the scapegoat in Vail, *Atonement and Salvation*, 126–28.

death—the most severe dismantling possible. He entered the not-created empty wilderness (*tohu wabohu*) for our sake. The Messiah and Savior of the world, through whom all things came to exist, put an end to all corruptions to re-create all things. He became undone (and, with him, all sin). Having entered death, he became the firstborn of the dead. He himself was the first word spoken out of the abyss. Through the one who created all things, all things are being made new. He was crucified according to the flesh—in creation's present experience of weakness, mortality, corruptibility—but he was raised in the fullness of the Spirit according to the everlasting life that all creation will enjoy in the coming age, in the fullness of divine life. In him, God has inaugurated a new way of existing that creation never had before.[33]

The cross appeared to be a total defeat and utter weakness, but it was the might of God's love on display, lifted up before the world. Rather than lose a single enemy or corrupted part of creation, to clear the way for creating new conditions, God accomplished the end of sin and death in Christ. He tasted death for everyone (Heb. 2:9). Now, we can be purified and made new through being united with Christ. Paul wrote, "I have been crucified with Christ and I no longer live, but Christ lives in me. The life I now live in the body, I live by faith in the Son of God, who loved me and gave himself for me" (Gal. 2:20).

Worldly messiahs—or, people promising some form of salvation—lose when they die. Death means they failed to deliver on their promise to rule or save. However, God's Messiah brings about God's reign and salvation for the world precisely by coming to an end in death in order to

---

33. See John Behr, "Nature, Wounded and Healed in Early Patristic Thought," *Toronto Journal of Theology* 29.1 (2013): 85–100, esp. 91–92; see Vail, "Making All Things New," *Eschatology*, 55–78.

bring resurrection life—new life. God gathers in the brokenness, suffering, and death so all things have the possibility of being re-created in the fellowship of divine love. Were it not for the resurrection, there would be no re-creation and, thus, no salvation (see Rom. 4:25; 2 Cor. 4:14). It is a great paradox that Christ has won redemption for us all by entering death, yet it is the act of new creation in the resurrection that brings forth salvation.

When Christ returns, the dead and the living will join him in the fullness of new creation life. The dead will be resurrected, and even those who are alive will be made new for everlasting life. Because all things will be under Christ, that will mean the end to every other "dominion, authority and power," including death itself (1 Cor. 15:24–27). Because of Christ, in Christ, through Christ, all things will be aligned under God "so that God may be all in all" (v. 28). The cross and resurrection are the way God cleanses and makes new without any deaths apart from God's own self-sacrifice. Through union with Christ in his death and resurrection, all creation can come to have that resurrection life within God's glory.[34] At the return of Christ, creation will be gloriously filled with God's loving presence, function according to God's wisdom, and be fully alive in the fellowship of the Father, Son, and Holy Spirit.

Because the disciples encountered the resurrected Christ, their despair turned to joy. They knew he was victorious as Redeemer-Creator-Ruler. "God exalted him to the highest place and gave him the name that is above every name, that at the name of Jesus every knee should bow, in heaven and on earth and under the earth, and every tongue acknowledge that Jesus Christ is Lord, to the glory

---

34. See Denis Edwards, "Sublime Communion and the Costs of Evolution," *Irish Theological Quarterly* 84.1 (2019): 22–38, esp. 27–28. On the significance of God's indwelling presence and the eternal purposes of God worked out through the incarnation of the divine Son, see Vail, *Atonement and Salvation*, 26–29.

of God the Father" (Phil. 2:9–11). Their knowledge could not be undermined, even when Stephen was killed under the existing authorities and "on that day a great persecution broke out against the church in Jerusalem, and all except the apostles were scattered throughout Judea and Samaria" (Acts 8:1). Instead of collapsing, "those who had been scattered preached the word wherever they went" (v. 4). The believers had received the seal of the Holy Spirit, "a deposit, guaranteeing what is to come" (2 Cor. 1:22; see 5:5)—that is, "the day of redemption" when Christ returns to finish the work of new creation, including the redemption of our bodies (Eph. 4:30; Rom. 8:23; see Eph. 1:13–14). Because the Spirit—the creative power of the resurrection—is at work in us, we "have tasted the goodness of the word of God and the powers of the coming age" (Heb. 6:5; see v. 4).[35]

Under each covenant, God's people have lived in the confidence of what God is doing and will do precisely because God has proven to be capable as Redeemer-Creator-Ruler. God has also proven to be faithful. There is no greater demonstration of God's love and faithfulness to creation and all humankind than being willing to suffer death in Christ Jesus for the salvation (re-creation) of God's prodigal, lost creation. All thanks and praise and glory be to the Father, in our Lord Jesus Christ, by the Holy Spirit!

---

35. See Frank D. Macchia, *Justified in the Spirit: Creation, Redemption, and the Triune God* (Grand Rapids: Eerdmans, 2010); Jürgen Moltmann, *Jesus Christ for Today's World* (Minneapolis: Fortress Press, 1995); D. Lyle Dabney, "'Justified by the Spirit': Soteriological Reflections on the Resurrection," *International Journal of Systematic Theology* 3.1 (2001): 46–68.

SEVEN | An Unfolding Tradition

There are many facets to explore in looking at how Christians have explained the doctrine of creation and understood the relationship between God and creation over Christianity's history. This chapter will examine several facets in Christianity's history. First, we will explore the rise of creation out of nothing. After this, the features of the doctrine as it matured in the second century will be clarified. Third, we will see some of the changes that took place in the way people thought over Christianity's history. Last, we will note some general features of our present context. In some ways, we live in a very exciting time. The overall picture of the universe that is painted in current scientific literature may have the most in common with biblical poetry about the world than any previous time in Christianity's history.

On the Way to *ex Nihilo*

The doctrine of "creation out of nothing" (in Latin, *creatio ex nihilo*) moved early to the foreground of Christian discussions about creation. There is a traceable progression toward second-century Christians completely stating the doctrine.

As noted in chapter 3, Genesis 1 is not explicit in saying *what* God creates *out of*. The text is written from a different cultural worldview than Western culture's focus on material and form. Even so, Genesis 1 has features that make it compatible with a *creatio ex nihilo* doctrine.[1]

First, God's creative work is comprehensive; it covers the whole of the heavens and the earth, all there is. God is universal Redeemer-Creator-Ruler.

Second, there were no prior heavens and earth to which anything could belong and from which God could draw. Before God's creative activities in verse 3, nothing exists as part of creation because God has not created its existence within the heavens and the earth. As far as God's creation is concerned, nothing existed yet.

Third, Genesis 1 breaks from many ancient Near Eastern narratives in which their gods mold primal materials into the different parts of the cosmos. Genesis 1 is silent about the materials God creates out of or the origin of the materials.

Fourth, the focus is on *making a new* (previously nonexistent) *situation*. Something is now the case that was not the case before—in this instance "a benevolent and life-sustaining order."[2]

While Genesis 1 is more interested in God instituting divine purposes for the functioning of a new situation,

---

1. If Genesis 1 was dogmatically straightforward on what to make of the first few verses, it would not have sparked so much debate in the rabbinic period. As it is, it "attracted a good deal of semantic, cosmological and mystical speculation" (Bockmuehl, "*Creatio ex nihilo* in Palestinian Judaism and Early Christianity," *Scottish Journal of Theology* 65.3 [2012]: 259). Its ambiguity may actually be one of its positive qualities. Susannah Ticciati suggests the ambiguity in the text of Genesis 1 has "potential for generativity" ("Anachronism or Illumination? Genesis 1 and Creation *ex nihilo*," *Anglican Theological Review* 99.4 [2017]: 695). This means the signs in the text have multi-valence and openness, so they have greater capacity to speak beyond the confines of its original context. Scripture can (indeed, must) "yield new, life-giving interpretations in changing contexts" (695–96). Out of this, Ticciati states: "The fact that the doctrine of creation *ex nihilo* was only crystallized and formulated a long time after the writing of Genesis 1 is not, therefore, an argument against its truthfulness as an interpretive perspective on Genesis 1" (699).

2. Bockmuehl quoting Jon D. Levenson, "*Creatio ex nihilo*," 263.

there is also room in the text for later readers to understand Genesis 1 in support of *creatio ex nihilo*. It is groundwork toward the doctrine.³

One supporting text in the progression toward an explicit doctrine of creation out of nothing is 2 Maccabees, written in the time period between the Old and New Testaments known either as the intertestamental or deuterocanonical period. Second Maccabees 7 recounts the story of a foreign king torturing and killing seven Jewish brothers and their mother because they would not renounce their faith and eat pork. One by one the brothers stood by their belief and hope in God, as Ruler of all, being able to raise the dead: "the King of the universe," declared one brother, "will raise us up to an everlasting renewal of life" (2 Macc. 7:9, NRSV; see v. 14). Even as the king was about to cut off another brother's tongue and hands, he proclaimed, "I got these [the tongue and hands] from Heaven . . . and from him I hope to get them back again" (v. 11, NRSV). Whether it was their body parts or their lives, the brothers knew God could give them back.

In her confession about the resurrection, their mother added statements about the mystery of her sons' creation and the creation of all things: "I do not know how you came into being in my womb. It was not I who gave you life and breath, nor I who set in order the elements within each of you. Therefore the Creator of the world, who shaped the beginning of humankind and devised the origin of all things, will in his mercy give life and breath back to you again, since you now forget yourselves for the sake of his

---

3. As Markus Bockmuehl says, "To be sure, the conceptual terminology of 'nothingness' came relatively late to Christians, and even later to Jews. Yet the substantive concern for God's free creation of the world without recourse to preexisting matter is repeatedly affirmed in pre-Christian Jewish texts, and constitutes perhaps the single most important building block for the emergence of an explicit doctrine of 'creation out of nothing'" (*"Creatio ex nihilo,"* 253; see 264).

laws" (vv. 22–23, NRSV).⁴ God gave them their existence in giving them life and shaping them. Though their mother did not know how God did that, she trusted that God could do it again through resurrection.

Following this, the mother made the most famous statement from the chapter: "I beg you, my child, to look at the heaven and the earth and see everything that is in them, and recognize that *God did not make them out of things that existed. And in the same way the human race came into being*" (v. 28, NRSV, emphasis added). On the basis of God's creative ability she told her last son, "Do not fear this butcher, but prove worthy of your brothers. Accept death, so that in God's mercy I may get you back again along with your brothers" (v. 29, NRSV). So long as they stayed faithful unto death, they believed God could and would redeem them.

The mother saw three things as parallel: God creating the cosmos not out of things that existed, the creation of humankind (including her sons), and resurrection from death. In birth and resurrection, something is coming to exist that did not exist before (at least in that form or condition). Birth and resurrection are not truly *creatio ex nihilo*, and they color what her statement about the creation of the cosmos means. That is, "if God makes 'out of non-being the things that are' this need not be *ex nihilo*."⁵ For example, someone could go to the beach and *create* sandcastles out of nonexistent sandcastles. Sandcastles now exist that did not exist before. In 2 Maccabees 7, the cosmos may not have existed (in that way) prior to God's activity, but it is not explicit (or implied by the connection to birth and resurrection) that nothing at all existed prior to God's creative activity. Also, keep in mind that the Bible sees God *creating*

---

4. See also the connections between Genesis 1:26–28; 4:1; and 5:1–3, where God's creation of humankind shares similar language to having babies.
5. Bockmuehl, "*Creatio ex nihilo*," 258; see 266, note 40.

anytime God makes a new situation come about, like redeeming people or the land. Thus, a statement such as this one about creation may not be exclusively about God's *first* creative act.

Romans 4:17 is the next text that supports the progression toward a doctrine of creation out of nothing. Like the mother in 2 Maccabees 7, Paul connects creation, offspring, and resurrection. Surrounded by statements about Abraham and Sarah being the origin of many nations (by both biology and faith), Paul refers to "the God who gives life to the dead and calls into being things that were not." Like 2 Maccabees 7, this statement also does not give us a full claim of there being nothing at all before God creates, especially given the interplay between the various topics in Romans 4. Offspring and resurrection are creative acts; a new situation comes to exist that was not the case before, even if it is not *ex nihilo*. Nevertheless, the language for a doctrine of creation out of nothing was beginning to emerge, and the first sprouts of the idea are there. As later theologians reflected on the doctrine and considered various implications, they expanded the idea of *nothing*, or *non-being*.

We should not pass too quickly over the detail that the two earliest statements explicitly moving toward creation *ex nihilo* are actually the basis for resurrection doctrine—our hope in God's total, ultimate redemption of our bodies from death. Israel regularly interwove redemption and creation in its writings. Thus, resurrection belongs within the same framework as creation. Two key doctrines grew up together. Just as believers were working out their beliefs about bodily resurrection from the grave, they were also introducing new language about creation, framing it as making "out of non-being the things that are" and calling "into being things that were not." This framing of creation gave persecuted Jews confidence that the "King of the universe" and "Creator of the world" could recreate missing body parts and restore life for the dead. Just as Paul wrote about God bringing a baby from Abraham's body that "was as good as dead" and Sarah's womb that "was also dead" (Rom. 4:19), he was able to move beyond resurrection as a mere hope and theory. He was among those who knew God had "raised Jesus our Lord from the dead" (v. 24; see also v. 25). When Paul wrote that God "calls into being things that were not," he connected it to a baby from Abraham and Sarah and to the certainty of Jesus's resurrection from the dead.[6]

The New Testament—especially Paul—sided with the way Judaism had started to summarize God's creative acts, in terms of making out of non-being. Writers were starting to use new language, and creation from non-being was becoming explicit. Even while moving in these directions, the unfolding doctrine of creation in Judaism and Christianity did not abandon its scriptural heritage. Instead, writers were clarifying which direction to interpret that scriptural heritage—that is, clarifying what the Hebrew Scriptures pointed toward. They interpreted the inherited tradition in the direction of creation out of nothing. Creation *ex nihilo* eventually became the consensus of what to say out of Scripture.[7] In one sense, then, it is *biblical* even if it is not explicitly spelled out in the Bible. The full doctrine is neither spelled out in the Bible nor is entirely an

---

6. In putting forward biblical support for the doctrine of creation out of nothing, appeals are also made to John 1:3; Colossians 1:16; and Hebrews 11:3. However, Bockmuehl represents where scholarship lands on these verses: "While we may all agree that such statements are *compatible* with God's sovereign creation out of nothing, what they actually affirm seems to be rather less than this" ("*Creatio ex nihilo*," 258; see 256–57).

7. See Paul Gavrilyuk's arguments about how the doctrine of creation out of nothing was normative in early Christianity ("Creation in Early Christian Polemical Literature: Irenaeus against the Gnostics and Athanasius against the Arians," *Modern Theology* 29.2 [2013]: 22–32). He overreaches in his claims about creation out of nothing becoming official orthodoxy in the fourth century. However, he is helpful in showing how Scripture and tradition formed together in early Christianity.

afterthought.[8] Early Christians held the doctrine as the summation of the Bible's teaching. *Creatio ex nihilo* is where Scripture led them as they tried to explain the faith in the second century.

Clarifying *ex Nihilo*

After the New Testament period, Christians continued to add clarifications to the doctrine. By the end of the second century, theologians had fully clarified that "nothing" means absolutely nothing—especially at the beginning. Heaven and earth did not exist. There was absolutely no material for God to work with (not even a darkness) and no space or time within which to work (no pit or vacuum). God was not *next to* or *in* this nothing, and there was *no time* in which God was not doing anything about the nothing. Any of those options would set up a dualism between an eternal God and an uncreated condition; they make the *no*thing into *some*thing to which God forever stands in relation.[9] They would also mean God's act of creation is built within, out of, or upon that thing that is supposed to be *nothing*. Instead, "the doctrine of creation out of nothing is precisely intended to deny that creation is *out of* anything—that is, that there is anything prior to creation that is either excluded by it, superseded by it, or imposed upon by it. There is nothing there to be excluded, superseded, or imposed upon."[10] Our triune Creator is without beginning and parallel. Everything else—visible and invisible—must be given existence by God, period. God created without reference to anything else. "The distinction between the

---

8. Bockmuehl, "*Creatio ex nihilo*," 269–70.
9. Ticciati, "Anachronism or Illumination?" 702–3.
10. Ticciati, "Anachronism or Illumination?" 703.

uncreated triune Godhead and the world created out of nothing became a normative part of the Christian faith."[11]

This full-blown version of the doctrine of creation out of nothing was in place by the end of the second century. Three people provided the key pieces. Tatian (AD 120–180) "is the first Christian theologian known to us who expressly advanced the proposition that matter was produced by God."[12] Earlier people may have said God creates out of nothing or non-being, like creating sandcastles on the beach. However, it was important to clarify that "create" includes making the material itself exist—especially in God's first creative acts. Tatian clarified that "creation" means God makes substance itself come into existence. He intentionally rejected the broader cultural worldview. "For the Greeks, the origin of the world was not *ex nihilo* but from material available in a formless or disordered state . . . [literally, a 'not-cosmos']."[13]

One step beyond Tatian is Theophilus of Antioch (died c. AD 181–190), who clarified that, when God creates out of nothing, God wills creation to happen. God is freely doing it. Also, since God is choosing to bring something into existence, God is not constricted "by the precondition of matter and its possibilities."[14] There is not too much or too little material. Matter also does not have bad properties with which God must contend, or properties that came about by fate, fortune, or outside pressures upon God. If God is choosing what to create out of nothing, God creates with "absolute unconditionality."[15] The very nature of material existence is according to God's wisdom, as God saw fit to

---

11. Gavrilyuk, "Creation in Early Christian Polemical Literature," 32.
12. May, *Creatio Ex Nihilo*, 150. See Brown, *Structure, Role, and Ideology*, 32–35.
13. Bockmuehl, "*Creatio ex nihilo*," 254f; see 255-257.
14. May, *Creatio Ex Nihilo*, 161.
15. May, *Creatio Ex Nihilo*, 163.

bring it into being. God has chosen this creation and blesses it with life and motion.

The final clarifications come from Irenaeus of Lyon (AD 130–202), who had a thoroughly Trinitarian description of God's creative activity throughout his work. God creates through God's "two hands"—the Word and the Spirit. As with the theologians who came before him, Irenaeus affirmed that God's creative actions are free and unbounded by any prior conditions. God chooses to bring forth material and the patterns for things; these come from God as God wills them.[16] When he says the patterns come *from God*, it may sound like Irenaeus is saying that God is the substance *out of* which creation is made. However, it is more that Irenaeus believed that God is not limited to preexisting ideas. The ideas are God's "intellectual property."[17] Yet even more, in creating, God communicates God's *will*—which "is Christ the Word of the Father"—who, in this divine self-communication of the Word, brings forth the world in divine goodness.[18] The Spirit is working here as well. The Spirit demonstrates the Word within creation, or arranges and forms, so that creation is adorned and furnished by the Spirit.[19] Creation is God's handiwork. The most natural way for creation to exist is within or according to God's own present will/Word and Spirit. Irenaeus did not speculate *how* God gives existence to things other than through the Word and Spirit. Creation is a *hands-on* activity

---

16. May, *Creatio Ex Nihilo*, 168–72.

17. May, *Creatio Ex Nihilo*, 173.

18. M. C. Steenberg, *Irenaeus on Creation: The Cosmic Christ and the Saga of Redemption* (Boston: Brill, 2008), 49.

19. See Steenberg, *Irenaeus on Creation*, 62–84. Before Irenaeus, Theophilus thought about the life-giving work of the Spirit in Genesis 1. The Spirit nourished the water so that "the water, together with the Spirit, might nourish the creation, penetrating it from all sides" (Steenberg, 89f.; Theophilus, *Ad Autolycum* 2.13).

that yields good results, as would be expected out of the direct engagement of our good Creator.

One of Irenaeus's clarifications with the idea that God is free and unconditioned in creating is that God did not have a need or deficiency that creation fills for God. God wills to start and sustain it. God wills to work all the way through, leading creation "toward redemption and final fellowship with himself."[20] God desired to have something beyond God's own triune being "to whom he could show his benevolence."[21] Creation is entirely a free gift. God's chosen gift of God's direct care is for creation to flourish in God's fellowship.

Scripture speaks of God's individualized care for each part of the world and each creature. Irenaeus follows in that line in talking about creation out of nothing. It is not just a blanket claim for Irenaeus that God popped a cosmos into existence in a sweeping, one-time act. Rather, "each existing entity has been called into existence from a state of nothingness, of non-being."[22] God has direct contact with every individual part of creation from its beginning and all the way into the fulfillment of God's purposes in creation.

The creative activity of God's will/Word and Spirit is ultimately shown in the Word taking flesh and dwelling among us and the Spirit coming to dwell in us. This is all part of the ultimate self-communication of God's goodness into and for the world so we can participate in the fellowship of the Father, Son, and Spirit. In other words, "God creates, that creation might participate in his glory, his goodness, which is that shared eternally by Father, Son and Spirit and exemplified by the Son's incarnate relationship to the Father through the Spirit in the economy of salva-

---

20. May, *Creatio Ex Nihilo*, 174.
21. May, *Creatio Ex Nihilo*, 175.
22. Steenberg, *Irenaeus on Creation*, 48.

tion."²³ We are created and re-created in the same freely chosen outpouring of God's love for the world.

Speaking of the World

Structures

What humankind observes about the universe, including our own planet, expands each day. New technologies help us see things unimaginably distant from us, things extremely small, things our five senses cannot detect, or even things in inaccessible, hidden places. The number and novelty of things we are discovering is both exciting and overwhelming. In addition, there seems to be no limit to what we can learn about the characteristics of various processes of physics, biology, chemistry, and more. We are nowhere close to saying we understand the entirety of God's creation. If anything, the multiplying information adds to our sense of wonder and humility. The world is so vast, and we are so small; some things last so long, and we are but a dot in time.

In the ancient Near East, the standard view of the cosmos was that there were the heavens and the earth—the dome of the sky and everything under our feet. The cosmos could also be divided three ways instead of two, like a three-layer cake: the heavens, the earth, and the watery abyss under the earth.

Eventually a Greek man named Ptolemy (c. AD 85–165) came up with his own geocentric (earth-centered) model of the cosmos based on observations and calculations that could predict the movements of objects in the heavens. Ptolemy placed earth in the middle of the cosmos with layers to the heavens around us—like the layers of an onion—going all the way out to the highest (outermost)

---

23. Steenberg, *Irenaeus on Creation*, 36.

heaven. Even though later observers needed to adjust his model, the Ptolemaic system lasted fourteen centuries.

From the 1500s to the early 1600s, people such as Copernicus, Kepler, and Galileo made observations and calculations that evaporated Ptolemy's geocentric model. Their discoveries demanded the adoption of a heliocentric (sun-centered) model.[24] Cosmic models have continued to change from the 1600s. They assumed a static, uniform three-dimensional space. In this stable space, objects exist and events take place over time. Einstein's twentieth-century theory of relativity and notion of space-time is just one example of our changing understanding.[25]

Writings

In every era, human beings had an idea of how they thought the cosmos was structured. They gave the most faithful account they could based on the information that was available. Even beyond describing cosmic structures, they would write about what the structures mean, why they are that way, and so forth. In our earliest records, humans gave those accounts about the cosmic structures—including how and why they are the way they are—through narratives and poetry. Even in the Old Testament we would be hard-pressed to find a statement about God, the cosmos, and the reasons for everything that is not in narrative or poetic form. The artistry of these forms draws us into wonder, allegiance, and praise, even as they instruct us in how we are meant to conduct ourselves in the world. We become participants in the narrative and poetic expressions. Inhabiting the text places our feet on a path.

---

24. Here is an explanation of the change from an earth-centered to sun-centered model: https://earthobservatory.nasa.gov/features/OrbitsHistory.

25. Stanford University has a helpful history on theories about space on their page "Gravity Probe B: Testing Einstein's Universe," https://einstein.stanford.edu/SPACETIME/spacetime1.html. Under the "SPACETIME" tab, there is information on "Before Einstein" and "Einstein's Spacetime."

It is not simply that we can track the history of people making different claims about the cosmos at different times. There has been a shift in how the claims are packaged and the intended function of the written accounts. Earlier texts—whose artistry was in service to religious purposes—gave way to more expository (informative) writing.[26] The Greek-minded Ptolemy explained what he saw. Centuries of Christians then wrote theology, prayers, and hymns thinking about God in what was the most accepted cosmic model. For example, during the era of the Ptolemaic model, Christians celebrated God, whose movements in the furthest heavenly realm gave movement all the way down to earth at what was perceived to be the cosmos's center.[27] For many centuries, Christians interwove their descriptions of the cosmos with their explanations of doctrine and their praises and prayers to God. They eventually built their churches to point heavenward while expecting the grace of God to flow down. Even though their writing was often expository, it tried to serve the holistic function that narrative and poetry had served: drawing readers into faithful living and praise of the Creator.

In the course of history, Christian writing came to serve functions that were more specialized. Some works, or sections of a work, could focus on explaining features of the cosmos. Some works or sections could explain doctrine. Sometimes the function could be prayer or praise. For example, in the twelfth century, Thierry of Chartres divided one of his works into two parts. In the first part,

---

26. This analogy may be a stretch, but Paul, for example, used a different writing style in his epistles than we see in Song of Solomon. Both authors talk about marriage and sex as faithfully as they know how, but Paul tends to *inform* his readers, and Song of Solomon directs readers toward a form of spousal love through art.

27. The website Before Newton offers one explanation of how Christians talked about God in Ptolemy' model: https://beforenewton.blog/daily-readings/september-9-medieval-european-cosmology/.

he explained the generation of the cosmos in line with the physics of his time: "in terms of the natural properties of the four material elements (earth, water, air, and fire)."[28] There was not heavy emphasis on God's activity in the first part. The second part of Thierry's work covers the scriptural and doctrinal explanations of God's creative work.[29]

For most of our history, Christians felt no tension between astronomy, physics, mathematics, or any other fields of study and what they believed concerning Scripture and Christian doctrine. As more science-like observations filled the Middle Ages, Christians still saw compatibility between *reading* the natural world and *reading* their Christian faith. They held them together without problem, seeing unity in all matters. During the medieval period, however, seeds were planted of a belief distinguishing between nature (or natural operations) and God's special interventions. Nevertheless, even when reflecting on the *natural* functions of the world, God was still in the equation: "the normal sequences of nature were viewed as due to a power delegated to nature by God."[30] God reliably sustained the operation of things through that avenue.

---

28. Christopher B. Kaiser, *Creational Theology and the History of Physical Science: The Creationist Tradition from Basil to Bohr* (New York: Brill, 1997), 50; Willemien Otten, "Nature and Scripture: Demise of a Medieval Analogy," *Harvard Theological Review* 88, no. 2 (1995): 269; José Morales, *Creation Theology* (Dublin: Four Courts Press, 2001), 56. Occasionally authors wrote about the unfolding of the world almost entirely in naturalistic ways. For example, William of Conches (died c. AD 1154) viewed the ordering of nature to be due to the inherent properties of the elements; nature orders and spawns itself (Kaiser, *Creational Theology*, 57).

29. Otten, "Nature and Scripture," 274–75.

30. Kaiser, *Creational Theology*, 54. The more that the functions of the world were observed, calculated, and described in ways that seemed to account for everything, the more God did not need to be mentioned. This worked its way into the general worldview of Western-minded people. Some people in the Middle Ages could go as far as thinking that *order* was not as much "upheld by God (through his word, will or power)" or seen *as* the work or vocation of God as it was due to the properties of matter (see Otten, "Nature and Scripture," 271).

During these middle centuries, some writers took personal interest in exploring the dependable operations of the world, and other writers had little interest in science. Thus, by the end of the Middle Ages, there were two wings in Christianity that emphasized different things in their writings—one emphasized natural processes under God's ordinary activity, and the other highlighted God's special, salvific interventions.[31] The drift into two wings of Christian writings happened gradually over seven centuries and shaped reflections on both sides. Theologians who gave less attention to nature began to emphasize less the biblical themes of God's salvation for the *whole* of creation and focused more on themes of *human* salvation.[32] Also, the more the world was seen as nature, or functioning according to natural law, the more it was viewed as impersonal and the more God's actions in the world seemed to be intrusive or disruptive to what is natural and normal.[33] It is not that one side was Christian and the other was not. Both wings saw themselves as Christian, and both sides came to suppose a world of nature into which God sometimes acted *super*naturally. Through the history of Christianity, science and faith were woven together, sometimes even in the careers of individual scholars. As late as the first half of the nineteenth century, it was common for some members of prestigious scientific groups, like the Royal Society of London, to be clergy.[34] Even though they may not be clergy, some of the leading scientists today have a robust Christian faith.

It is sad that the theological imagination of Western culture started to drift into separated realms of a natural world and God's supernatural interjections. Thomas Aquinas provided a theological framework that kept the two sides together at least from the 1200s to the 1600s.

31. Kaiser, *Creational Theology*, 52–54.
32. Otten, "Nature and Scripture," 282.
33. Kaiser, *Creational Theology*, 54–55.
34. Kaiser, *Creational Theology*, 367; see The Royal Society, https://royalsociety.org/about-us/.

The Scriptures marvel at the world around us.

To a large degree, science was birthed within and out of the Christian heritage that long dominated the West. The Scriptures marvel at the world around us. They speak of God's great, tender-loving care in how all things work together according to God's great wisdom. Scripture invites readers to take note of the fine details, and Christians have been taking note! With today's technologies, we can observe even further the ways the world and its inhabitants are responding within God's life-giving activity. We can also better understand and practice our own God-given vocation as priests in God's sanctuary—mediating God's blessings for the well-being of the earth and its inhabitants. Listening to the world and our fellow creatures through scientific study can be one of the greatest aids there is to loving our neighbor (all creation) as ourselves. Through careful examination we understand better the way things work, hear where creation is groaning, and respond in helpful ways as God's children (Rom. 8:18–25). Christianity ought to keep to its roots in keeping all dimensions of life in the world (including our intellectual and scientific pursuits) in service to our God-given vocation, that the glory of God's love may shine in us and through us in tending and keeping God's sanctuary.

Theological Imagination

The Nicene Creed starts by affirming the Father as "maker of heaven and earth, of all that is, seen and unseen." The Creed also declares the Son as the one through whom "all things were made" and the Spirit as "the Lord, the giver of life." It is not hard to find biblical passages that support God's all-encompassing role as Creator: "Through him all things were made; without him nothing was made that has been made" (John 1:3). God as Creator has remained constant from the Old Testament on through each era of the Christian tradition. Other things have changed, like what it means to create, the structure of the world God creates, how

God creates, God's imagined relationship to the world, creation's relationship to God, and many other things.

We have already seen some of these things to this point. Here are some of the ways the definition of "create" changed. Scripture contains many different words for God's creative acts: making, forming, breathing, speaking, naming, establishing, and so on. These terms do several things. First, they place God on location. God is immediately present. Second, they depict God as directly, almost physically, active—especially when authors employ imagery from different skilled crafts. Third, God's creative work takes time. Many of these actions are not done in a flash. Some things God works to establish in Scripture take a long time to unfold and come to fruition, like giving Abraham and Sarah innumerable descendants. Fourth, creation is not a past activity that only happened once, at a beginning point. God's governance of all things entails continual creative acts. God's interaction with creation, as Ruler, creates new circumstances for the world (providing, guiding, renewing, and sometimes cleaning house). We are looking forward to God's ultimate creative act of fulfilling God's purposes for all things at Christ's return. Fifth, because God's role of Creator is tied to God's position as Ruler, God's creative activities include obedience and responsiveness from God's subjects. While the Creator-Ruler initiates, the desired result requires obedient participation from God's creation, often an ongoing obedience—like the earth producing vegetation and humans tending and keeping. In any kingdom, the ruler is not singlehandedly doing all the work.

In the first four centuries of Christianity, many of these things changed. At first, when Jews and Christians said God creates out of non-being, few of those five features were affected. When God works as Creator-Ruler, there is a result that did not exist before. However, by the second century, there were overarching conversations about the origin and nature of material existence. Specifically there were questions on: (1) whether matter had no origin and eternally existed with God, and (2) whether material was inherently a bad or inferior way to exist, which would make our ultimate hope escaping the physical realm to become unchangeable spirits. Second-century Christians used the tradition they had—specifically, God creates from what did not exist—to answer both questions. Matter is not eternally with God in a dualistic relationship. God alone is uncreated, and matter has a beginning point when it is created by God *ex nihilo*. In answer to the second question, they affirmed that God makes good things. Thus, the material world is not inherently bad. Our goal is not to escape physical existence. Rather, we look for the resurrection of our bodies from the grave and God's transformation of all creation in the fullness of God's indwelling presence.

This conversation affected Christianity's imagination about the meaning and scope of "create." If creating required producing matter, then God does not do this over the lifetime of a person, people group, or all creation. It happens only at the beginning point of any given thing's existence. Initially in the second century, there was still conversation about God producing the material in a raw state and then forming it. That kept some of the idea that God's creative activity unfolds over time. However, when Irenaeus said God produces the material in a formed state, he reduced God's creative activity to the beginning moment of something coming into existence. Any subsequent ways that God interacted with the world or changed things was not an act of creation. Irenaeus meant to highlight God's direct contact with every individual creation by saying God created each one *ex nihilo*. However, in the eighteen centuries since then, conversation about God *creating* has typically been limited to the beginning moment of God giving existence to space, time, and material—or, at the most, to conversation about the Genesis 1 narrative of seven days.

Creatio ex nihilo has not required us to imagine God's intimate engagement in creative processes that take time or happen over creation's entire timespan. It is also not as clear how this creative act of giving being is logically inseparable from God being Ruler and Redeemer. In Christian history, Christians still understood God as Creator and Ruler. However, God *created* (in the beginning), and now God *governs* what God made.[35] The emphasis on creation out of nothing also limited the range of divine activities in Scripture that fall within God's creative work. "Create" came to be synonymous with "giving existence or being." God came to be understood for centuries as Being—the uncreated, unoriginated one who has existence in God's self. God as Being gives *being* to all there is.[36] These shifts corresponded with the expansion of ideas about God's timelessness and God never experiencing any change.

To be fair, Christians were doing their best to explain Christianity faithfully in a world that thought differently about the cosmos and divinity than Judaism. During early Christianity, the context of the Roman Empire had a Ptolemaic cosmology partnered mostly with platonic-based philosophies about the nature of divinity and material existence.[37] When platonic philosophy lost its seat to Aristotle's

---

35. Irenaeus, at the end of the second century, was keeping God's activities toward creation as part of a single relationship God has with the world as Redeemer-Creator-Ruler. Steenberg does a great job demonstrating this single connected narrative of God with creation in *Irenaeus on Creation: The Cosmic Christ and the Saga of Redemption*. The title alone suggests continuity from the dawn of creation into creation's full participation in the glory of God.

36. D. Lyle Dabney, "The Nature of the Spirit: Creation as a Premonition of God," *Starting with the Spirit*, ed. Stephen Pickard and Gordon Preece (Adelaide, Australia: Openbook Publishers, 2001), 92.

37. See Donald Zeyl and Barbara Sattler, "Plato's *Timaeus*," *Stanford Encyclopedia of Philosophy*, December 18, 2017, https://plato.stanford.edu/entries/plato-timaeus/.

philosophy in the 1200s, God was explained in light of Aristotle's First Mover in that new cultural context.

The end result of these centuries of translating Christianity was a way of imagining a distinction between the realm of nature and the realm of God.[38] At the end of the Middle Ages, God seemed even more hands-off when some theologians used the analogy of God being a clockmaker who did not have to act continually for natural mechanisms to click along with almost total independence.[39] With the imagined distances between *when* God acted or *where* God resided, Christians imagined that the purpose of human beings was to find fulfillment "by ascending to God through . . . an infusion of the grace."[40] The church helped mediate the distance between God in the highest heaven and the natural world. Certainly creation operated by grace, but we would need further grace to transcend natural virtues to the theological virtues of faith, hope, and love. In the relationship between Creator and creation, the existence of *nature* (by grace) was simply presupposed; it was then added onto or perfected by more grace.[41] In many ways, just as a division had opened between God as Creator

---

38. Kaiser, *Creational Theology*, 104. Aquinas in the 1200s tried to keep this divide from taking place (Otten, "Nature and Scripture," 282; see Kaiser, *Creational Theology*, 93–94).

39. Kaiser, *Creational Theology*, 106, 109. Otten notes that by the late medieval period God's volitional actions were no longer reflected in the workings of nature ("Nature and Scripture," 264). The study of nature for the purpose of attempting to know God more richly dissipated. Romans 1:20 had been a favorite proof-text throughout the Middle Ages: "Ever since the creation of the world his eternal power and divine nature, invisible though they are, have been understood and seen through the things he has made" (NRSV). However, the logic of medieval theology became severed; they could no longer believe God's agency was reflected in creation and could be imperfectly grasped by humans (Otten, "Nature and Scripture," 265). The Reformation's emphasis on original sin added even more reasons why Christians did not think creation reflected God's will.

40. Dabney, "Starting with the Spirit: Why the Last Should Now Be First," *Starting with the Spirit*, 17.

41. Dabney, "Starting with the Spirit," 18.

and Ruler, so also a division opened up in God as Creator and God's acts of redemption. Creator, Ruler, and Redeemer became their own separate plotlines—the story of making the world, the story of ruling the world, and the story of saving and fulfilling the world. They belonged to different doctrines and to different times or dimensions in creation's relation with God. Redeemer, Creator, and Ruler were no longer inseparable divine functions of God all the way from beginning to fulfillment.

Thoughts about God as Creator continued to change after the middle ages. During the Reformation, God's creative work was framed less in terms of God (Being) giving existence and more in terms of God's Word establishing the world according to God's sovereign will. God declares it singlehandedly. Since the Reformation, it is still common to hear people explain God's creative work almost exclusively as God *speaking* the world into existence *ex nihilo*. "God said" is sometimes the only divine creative action some readers list from Genesis 1. Speaking the world *ex nihilo* reinforced the notion that creation is only a topic about the beginning. In addition, creation's goodness was confined to the beginning of the story in many Christians' imaginations because of a surging emphasis on the world's fallenness. Whatever God did in creating is a matter of the past, and the world is something else now. Within this Reformation worldview, there was a sense that in Christ, God (as Redeemer) was *confronting* human beings and their sin (unlike as Creator). "The Redeemer Jesus Christ as the Divine Word stands over and against creation"—coming at us from outside.[42] The sin of the world stands in sharp distinction to God, like night and day. God must descend to the world in Christ and impute a righteousness to us that is foreign to

---

42. Dabney, "Starting with the Spirit," 20.

us.[43] There is no creation *and* God, nature *and* grace. There is no continuum, only contradiction between the world and its Creator.[44] Furthermore, just as God's role as Creator was confined to its place in time, redemption was not the same thing as God's normal function within the world as Ruler. Redemption was a separate action.[45]

It did not take long into the Modern period for perspectives to fragment in many different directions, to the point where it is difficult to describe a dominant Western or Christian perspective. In general, theology was still included in people's explanations of the universe. Early on, some people believed God acted at the beginning as a designer or lawgiver, and now nature operated entirely on account of those God-given mechanics.[46] Other people still described spiritual energies at work in the world as a residual effect of God's initial divine decree.[47] A new version of Platonism also came up in which they thought some type of spirit or world soul permeated all things to influence matter.[48] The first two groups did not see much need for continual divine activity in the world. The last group could only survive public scrutiny as long as scientific formulas could not ac-

---

43. Dabney, "Starting with the Spirit," 20.

44. Dabney, "Starting with the Spirit," 20.

45. Interestingly the Reformers generally preferred the Aristotelian view of the cosmos and its ordered structures, as well as the notion of *potentia ordinata* (God's ordinary, governing power) that was stressed within the later Middle Ages (Kaiser, *Creational Theology*, 177). However, whereas the Middle Ages tension was between nature (*potentia ordinata*) and supernature (God's absolute, saving power), the Reformers created a new division in the *potentia ordinata* and focused on the dialectic between creation and salvation ordinances (177). Nature and grace were no longer divided between the arenas of God's *ordinary power* and God's *absolute power*. Instead they were both discussed under two distinct kinds of *ordinary power*.

46. Kaiser, *Creational Theology*, 234.

47. Kaiser, *Creational Theology*, 212.

48. Kaiser, *Creational Theology*, 237.

count for the various forces in physics and the movement of material objects in the universe.[49]

In the 1600s, Baruch Spinoza introduced a fourth, non-spiritual option. He reduced everything divine and spiritual to the material. He claimed that what had always been attributed to God, or was due to influences from a spiritual dimension, is what happens *naturally*, based on properties and motions inherent in matter.[50] "God" is some feature within the universe. What you see is what you get. There is no divine power *beyond* exactly what is happening in the world.[51] There is nothing transcendent to the physical universe that supersedes the sum of its inner working. This view now undergirds Western imagination.

---

49. With time, due to the growing confidence in the scientific method, no one "any longer resorted to Newton's God-of-the-gaps to account for the unresolved problems" (Kaiser, *Creational Theology*, 346). Gaps were considered a matter of ignorance and not a place for divine activity.

50. Jonathan Israel, *Enlightenment Contested: Philosophy, Modernity, and the Emancipation of Man, 1670–1752* (New York: Oxford University Press, 2006), 433; see Cyril O'Regan, "Spinoza and the Eclipse of Creation from Nothing," *Creation ex nihilo*, 233–273. Spinoza did not think there could be "some form of causal mediation between the immaterial God and material world" (O'Regan, 237). Spinoza wondered how something that has nothing in common with something else could be its cause. He went back to the ancient Greek truism that *like comes from like*. "One substance cannot be produced by another substance" (O'Regan, 237).

51. O'Regan, "Spinoza and the Eclipse of Creation from Nothing," 246. Many early Americans, like Thomas Jefferson and Benjamin Franklin, used the word "God" when they meant the processes of nature. This position is what O'Regan calls "natural supernaturalism." It "allows nature or the world to have some self-transcendent momentum beyond what can be accounted for by science." At the same time, it rejects the God of Judaism and Christianity, along with the world being created by that God (O' Regan, "Spinoza and the Eclipse of Creation from Nothing," 234). By using the term "God," many American founders could hide their lack of belief in plain sight in a culture where belief was the expected norm (see Matthew Stewart, *Nature's God: The Heretical Origins of the American Republic* [New York: W. W. Norton & Co., 2014]).

Where Are We?

When the presiding philosophy or scientific models changed over the last two thousand years, Christians found themselves explaining their faith anew within each new cultural context. Christians worked within the various contexts, even while many of their beliefs challenged those cultural frameworks.[52] Whether Christians were making statements within a cultural context or in response to debates among fellow Christians, the contexts and conversations through that history affected the way Christianity came to talk about its beliefs.[53]

The last three centuries have been especially hard for Christians to navigate. Western culture as a whole has wanted verifiable evidence to support any claims, and found it in abundance in the sciences. God's existence and activity, however, are not testable hypotheses within the methods of science. Nevertheless, many Christians have continued in the path of Christianity's history and

---

52. See May, *Creatio Ex Nihilo*, xii and 164 onward.

53. Here is one example. Steven Baldner and William Carroll, in the introduction to their translation of Aquinas's writings on creation, claim that, for Augustine and Aquinas, "what is essential to the Christian faith is the fact of creation, not its manner or mode" (*Aquinas on Creation: Writings on the "Sentences" of Peter Lombard 2.1.1* [Toronto: Pontifical Institute of Mediaeval Studies, 1997], 3f). What Baldner and Carroll mean by "creation" is explained further: "The explanation of the six days is really an account of the *formation* of the world, not its *creation*" (4). The primary question of philosophy during that era was existence—our dependence on God, who is Being. Thus, the time period itself shaped the question(s) theology answered concerning the topic of creation. "Thus questions such as, how does the first cause give being (existence) to creatures, and how do creatures receive the being that is given to them, are central to such an investigation" (4). Later, as knowledge of the world became of highest significance, interest in God's creative involvement in the six days again became part of treatments on *creation*. Only secondarily did later thinkers ask if God was necessary to start the causal unfolding they observed. Even back in the twelfth century scientists had already started taking the beginning of the world for granted and focused on explaining the beauty of the world (Otten, "Reading Creation," 243).

kept their conviction about God being the Redeemer-Creator-Ruler of all things, while marveling at all that the sciences are discovering about the history and workings of God's world. As Christians have always done, they continue to give an account of God and the world in their current context. Again, Christian convictions cannot be tested and proven using the methods of science. It is by the gracious working of God that we enter into faith.[54] This does not mean that Christians' viewpoint is irrational or that they cannot offer an account of the faith in a context full of scientific discoveries.

Christians have struggled to know how to engage the conversation of the broader culture in ways that hold weight. There is the added challenge of keeping up with where the conversation is located as the broader culture and scientific discovery continue to move at increasing speed. Christians have to keep communicating to an ever-changing world. Even so, our context is full of promise. In the last three hundred years, the dead, mechanistic view of the universe has given way to a world full of interactions and surprises.[55] During a good portion of the Modern era, Western culture assumed the world was a dead backdrop for our human story and raw material resource we could change and use for our own gains. However, the lifeless, mechanistic view of the world has given way to something far more lively. "Billiard-ball physics has no basis in reality."[56]

---

54. Christians hold our beliefs through the Holy Spirit at work in us (John 3:5; 1 Cor. 2:1–16); apart from the Spirit's activity, the kingdom of God will look unwise and foolish to people. It is not that Christian theology is irrational; the church across history has examined and clarified its beliefs. Rather, faith is the starting point. Faith perpetually seeks further understanding.

55. Arnold Benz, *The Future of the Universe: Chance, Chaos, God?* (New York: Continuum, 2000), 135.

56. Jeffrey S. Wicken, "The Cosmic Breath: Reflections on the Thermodynamics of Creation," *Zygon* 19.4 (1984): 501. See T. F. Torrance, *Divine and Contingent Order* (Oxford: Oxford University Press, 1981), 99–102. In science, traditional notions of cause ended. There is now the view about a contingent (re-

Somehow particles are interlocked and "communicate" over distances. Rather than simple cause and effect, there is "an ingredient of self-determination by a material nature that impresses its own identity on whatever processes proceed through it."[57] The interaction among things can bring about new kinds of arrangements and conditions beyond straightforward cause and effect. Even non-organic things are not simply existing through time in a deterministic line of cause-and-effect events. Also, context matters. Einstein's ideas about differences in space-time have rewritten earlier ideas about uniformity of space. "One cannot derive ordered phenomena, the units of individuality, from blind motions. . . . They are always conditioned or informed by macroscopic context."[58] We cannot know how things will bounce around and end up later. Complex, context-specific, irreversible interactions are the norm.[59]

During the infancy of scientific methods, it was common to put a specimen on a table and look at every detail

---

lational) order in which all things are intrinsically interdependent; contingence is about relationships. "Such is the vast change effected by relativity physics: classical causal relations are replaced by a dynamic inherent relatedness in the universe, in which space and time are included within the internal connections of all empirical realities and processes and are inseparable from them as spacetime. Mechanical laws are discarded along with the rigid structure of classically defined space and time, and field laws are formulated instead, which describe the dynamic invariances of space-time as an orderly open continuum of contingent realities and events" (Torrance, 100).

57. Wicken, 502; see Ilya Prigogine and Isabelle Stengers, *Order Out of Chaos: Man's New Dialogue with Nature* (New York: Bantam Books, 1984), 12. Benz discusses in a helpful section what science means by "self-organization" when there technically is no "self" (see Benz, 136ff.). In short, it refers to systems that organize in ways independent of initial conditions—i.e., they do not unfold according to a linear causal chain from initial conditions (136).

58. Wicken, 502.

59. "In the church's reflections on creation, the beginning gained ever-increasing importance. More and more in science, however, subsequent events are constitutive of the present and future system or thing. Beginnings are only just that, beginnings. Contemporary work on creation theology should be sensitive to this matter" (Vail, *Creation and Chaos Talk*, 56, note 175).

in order to figure out the nature of the thing. Items were examined out of context, and organic specimens were often dead. Things, however, are part of systems; they function in relation to the things around them.

> A system is characterized by more than its present state; the path taken also counts, the process is part of the product. . . . This world is one where nature is inherently historical, where matter at even the inanimate level displays an indelible sense of evolution. . . . The character of the present is dependent on the path from the past: although 'all roads lead to Rome,' the actual journey influences the quality of arrival. It is a world in fluctuation, filled with novelty.[60]

Scientists have made great strides in understanding whole ecosystems and how all the pieces work together—as well as the damage caused when things are out of balance. Here are some examples. When the USA created the national park system, there was a period when rangers shot predators in order to keep prey-animal populations high. This practice, however, left large herds of plant-eating animals. Since they no longer needed to keep moving to avoid predators, they were able to remain stationary and overgraze everything from saplings along waterways to undergrowth in forests. The lack of predators degraded the landscape. Similar problems showed up in the marine environment off the Aleutian Islands when sea otters were overhunted. This overhunting allowed sea urchins—one of the otters' food sources—to turn the ocean bottom into a wasteland. Finally, when the national parks' boundaries were set, they

---

60. Robert John Russell, "Entropy and Evil," *Zygon* 19.4 (1984): 451. See the way systems are more of the basic unit than a lone specimen, whether in the natural sciences or social sciences; see, e.g., Joseph Bracken, *Society and Spirit: A Trinitarian Cosmology* (Selinsgrove, PA: Susquehanna University Press, 1991); and Edwin Friedman, *Generation to Generation: Family Process in Church and Synagogue* (New York: The Guilford Press, 1985).

typically encompassed the most beautiful areas. Scientists did not yet understand how the park itself was connected to the surrounding lands as one ecosystem. When lands outside the boundaries of the parks were developed, the stress and damage to those environments rippled into the park systems that depended on the interrelationship. The Yellowstone basins, for example, were known for their massive herds of elk and bison. However, those herds migrate to lower elevations outside the park boundaries at different times in the year for food. If their routes are cut off or they are not protected from hunting when they are outside park boundaries, the strength of those herds and the role they play in Yellowstone National Park are diminished.

Many of the changes in scientific understanding are welcome news for Christians. Nature is not simply a lifeless stage upon which we act out human history; it is not rightly called a "natural resource," nor can it be confined to or summarized by universal claims. "The great founders of Western science stressed the universality and the eternal character of natural laws. They set out to formulate general schemes that would coincide with the very ideal of rationality."[61] However, humankind is finding that the world is far more fuzzy than can be calculated according to deterministic, linear processes. It is more alive than that.

As Christians reflect on the confession that God is the Creator of the heavens and the earth, these new discoveries about the world raise new questions. In the Modern Era, people thought God set up laws or built a machine but could then be uninvolved. The beginning seemed to define everything that followed. Now it seems like the beginning does not settle everything. Perhaps in our present context there is room again for the kind of personification of the world that we see in the Bible. Maybe creation is respond-

---

61. Prigogine and Stengers, 1.

ing to God's call to put forth vegetation and support birds, fish, and land animals. Maybe it is doing a range of things like glorifying its Creator, groaning because of our abuses, or failing to fulfill its purpose—like the fig tree that Jesus cursed on the way into Jerusalem because it had no fruit (Matt. 21:18–20). Maybe God has been operating as Redeemer-Creator-Ruler all the way along and the waters and earth are functioning in response to God's present activity. This may be one of the most exciting times for Christians to be in dialogue with the natural sciences. There may be more in common now between what science is saying and how Scripture characterizes the relationship between Creator and creation than there has been in many centuries.

EIGHT

Creation Imagination

The doctrine of creation matters in daily living. As we saw earlier, the people of Israel worked out the doctrines of salvation, creation, and resurrection in times of trial. Jesus's followers also experienced trials in the Roman Empire and clung to these doctrines. The doctrine of creation can assure us of God's place in the world. At the same time, God's character makes all the difference in performing the role of Creator. God's intentions for the world also factor significantly. God's character and intentions give specific shape to our daily living. Doctrine matters for perspective and life practice.

The goal of this chapter is not to repeat everything that has already been said. The previous chapters provide the necessary foundation for imagining the doctrine of creation in this chapter, but before we unpack that picture, there are two challenges in front of the doctrine of *creatio ex nihilo* that need to be explained. One of the challenges is Christianity's struggle to explain the relationship between God and creation—how creation is dependent on God but distinct from God. The other challenge addresses how the doctrine of creation should highlight the *reciprocal* relationship of love between God and creation, instead of making God the only actor—including being the author of bad things. With those challenges clarified, we can imagine the doctrine in our twenty-first-century context.

Challenge One:
Tensions over Agency and Existence

Western-minded people tend to ask who is responsible for things.[1] We want to know the cause—who should be praised or blamed. Within the doctrine of creation, we may wonder if our experiences in the world are due to something God did (or wanted), or something done by another agent. In the history of Christianity, we have wrestled with this question in several ways, usually in conversation with the broader culture with which Christians have engaged.

Greco-Roman thinking (that early Christians engaged) had its own ideas about the nature of divinity. One of them was that divinity could lack nothing. God was always complete. For instance, there is no time when the divine being could ever *not* be doing every action that divinity does. If at any time the divine being was not entirely active, then it would lack total divinity. This was the same for thinking and willing. All thoughts and things divinity wills have to be continuously thought and willed for all eternity. Power was included too. If divinity was not always fully exercising every capacity, then its power would be deficient, and that god would not really be *god*. Even more unthinkable, if anything other than deity ever contributed to divine activity, then the divine being would be deficient in that instance by receiving help.[2] They used zero-sum accounting, in which anything that one side does subtracts from the other person's side of the balance sheet; all activity had to be on God's side of the ledger. Divinity can never be incomplete.

---

  1. This is not true of every culture. See, for example, Lera Boroditsky's lectures, "How Language Shapes the Way We Think," https://youtu.be/RKK7wGAYP6k and "Beyond Words?" https://youtu.be/LYV3AYzhAzc.

  2. Western culture has long worshiped the idol of independence and self-sufficiency. See Severson, *Scandalous Obligation*, 141–43, 151–57.

Early Christians explained their beliefs to their Greco-Roman neighbors. *Creatio ex nihilo* helped them show that God has no deficiencies. God does not need existing materials or ideas in order to make the world; God is able to do the work entirely alone. It also helped them talk about God freely choosing to create—willing the character of physical existence. Created existence was inherently good and also distinct from divinity. The constant challenge for Christians, however, has been to explain when or how God's sole activity ends. In other words, how are the things that happen in creation ever not entirely due to the power and will of God? Is God the one who makes everything happen—both good and bad? Conversation with the Greco-Roman world kept pushing Christian thought toward God as the only agent. Under this issue of agency, there are two major ways Christians have explained how God gives existence to creation. When first engaging the Greco-Roman perspective, Christians explained that God is *Being* and gives the world its *being*. Moving from God's Being to the world's being was a good way to emphasize creation's goodness and to show that all things depend on God for their existence. If God no longer willed or supported something's existence, it would cease to exist.

The challenge was how to explain always receiving existence from God, while also saying that the world is distinct from God—existing as an agent separate from God. On one hand, Christianity did not want to merge the world into God. The world is not an extension of God. There is no direct continuity of being from God's being to creation. God and creation are not at two ends of the same continuum—with divinity at the highest end and creaturely existence at the lowest end. God and creation exist in different ways—one uncreated, the other created. On the other hand, Christianity insists that God is not to be separated from the world. God sustains and enlivens creation. The world does not have existence in itself, with no need of God. God is not a foreign intruder who occasionally interrupts an independent world.³ So explaining how God creates and sustains the world, while protecting creation's proper distinction from God's own being, was a challenge.

It was no easier to describe creation's *dependence on* and *distinction from* God when Christianity turned toward saying that God "spoke" creation into being.⁴ In this framework, in what way does God's will or Word become manifest in the world? If what God speaks into existence comes to be, it then seems that God's Word takes shape *as* creation—as the material world. God's declaration seems to have taken form as the thing God willed. God speaking the world into existence would not be a problem if God's speaking were impersonal. However, Christianity affirms that the Second Person of the Trinity—the eternal Word of God—is the one through whom God created and creates (John 1:1–5; Col. 1:15–17). We certainly do not want that divine Word to *become* the physical world itself—its substance or form. The *in*carnation of the Word in Christ is profound and unique. Christ is God's own self-expression operating in the world, as creaturely existence itself. But as Creator, the Word does not *become* the world. In turn, the world does not express the Word.

This challenge of distinguishing between divine and creaturely *agency* and between divine and creaturely *being* remains. Often we have wrongly separated the doctrine of creation from doctrines addressing God's continuing activity in the world. We made God's creative work entirely God's act at the beginning point. Then, when God sustains,

---

3. Since the Middle Ages, creation's continual dependence on God has progressively slipped from Christians' everyday thinking and living.

4. Creation by sovereign dictate progressively filled theological thinking through the Middle Ages and dominated from the Reformation onward. Natural and moral law became key categories across several doctrines.

provides for, and saves the world, God works with an active world. We need coherence.

Challenge Two: Mutual, Reciprocal Love

This second challenge could be seen as a recent repackaged expression of the first challenge. However, it especially relates to people who identify with the Wesleyan theological tradition. First, some Wesleyan theologians believe *creatio ex nihilo* backs us into saying God is the lone actor who causes everything in the world—including bad things. Explanations of *creatio ex nihilo* often depict God's action as absolute and unquestionable. In other words, God brings all things into being exactly as God sovereignly wills them. Is it God's doing if creatures are born with a sickness or abnormality? Does everything come into being as it does because God spoke it into being or willed it that way? Do all problems lie at God's feet? Creation out of nothing might connect every issue in the world to God's sovereign will.

Even if we want to say that problems are due to the world being fallen, God would still be bringing things into existence in that fallen form. Somehow, it would appear, God is creating a not-good world, while God is also working to redeem creation and wills for it to operate in love. God would be a divided house, willing and doing contradictory things. There are some traditions within Western Christianity that are content to say God brings things into existence in a broken state as punishment for everyone's guilt in original sin. However, Jesus seems to dismiss connecting birth defects with punishment for sin (John 9). Creation of all things by the sole will and power of God does not leave much room for creaturely responsibility for the ills in the world. It makes good and bad the result of God's will and work.

Second (and more to the heart of some Wesleyan concerns), if God created *ex nihilo*, that would be an authoritarian act and would violate a loving, reciprocal relationship between God and creation.[5] If these theologians are correct about creation out of nothing, it would contradict the core of Wesleyan thinking that love is God's central attribute (God's very nature). We have highlighted that God's role as Ruler is done according to God's loving nature. God's function as Redeemer-Creator-Ruler is not God's essential character. These are not eternal attributes, since creation has a beginning. Love is God's essential, eternal nature. Love is God's mode of operating as Redeemer-Creator-Ruler.

As a consequence of saying that all things result from God's action, *creatio ex nihilo* typically lacks creaturely response to God's initiative. In the beginning, it excludes mutual, reciprocal love between God and creation. If God is love, as God's most central attribute, this totalizing act would contradict God acting in loving, mutual relation with God's creation. Note here that this accusation against creation out of *nothing* is suggesting that, in the beginning, God is acting on or against *nothing*, which sounds like a contradiction of logic.[6] Nevertheless, we need an account of creation out of nothing that allows for creaturely dependence on and difference from God. At the same time, the doctrine of creation should be able to account for divine-creaturely love, rather than be framed as an exclusively divine dictate. God's way of creating should be consistent with what God wants creation to be and how it is meant to function.

---

5. For a helpful window into positions that support creation out of nothing and reject it, see Thomas Jay Oord, ed., *Theologies of Creation: Creatio Ex Nihilo and Its New Rivals* (New York: Routledge, 2014). See also Nathan Chambers, "Divine and Creaturely Agency in Genesis 1," *Scottish Journal of Theology* 72.1 (2019): 1–19.

6. Susannah Ticciati thinks this accusation against creation out of nothing breaks the rule of creation *out of nothing* by making the nothing into something that God violates ("Anachronism or Illumination?" 702–3).

God's way of creating should be consistent with what God wants creation to be and how it is meant to function.

A Wesleyan Account of *Creatio ex Nihilo*

We should begin by clarifying that creation out of nothing does not summarize the doctrine of creation; it is *one part* of the *whole* doctrine. God may have begun creating from nothing. However, God's creative actions are diverse in Scripture, and not every creative act is strictly *ex nihilo*. Scripture teaches that God creates across time—not just at the beginning—and much of that is not out of absolute nothing. Once there is space, time, and matter, it is not logically necessary for every creative act after that to be *ex nihilo*. Christianity actually rejects the idea that God's redemptive work is a new creation *ex nihilo*. It is the very thing that is broken and in need of salvation that is made new (saved)—like being resurrected from the grave. Without redemptive recreation, we are not saved; we are lost to sin and death. Perhaps, when dividing loaves and fish to feed the multitudes, Jesus brought forth material that was not already in the original loaves and fish. Thus, even now, God's creative capacities supersede the finite limitations of the heavens and the earth. Nevertheless, the Bible does not back us into the claim that every creative act must be generated *ex nihilo* in the absolute sense.

Early Christians were operating within the philosophical context of the Greco-Roman world, and we can applaud them for their good work of communicating in categories their audience could tolerate and understand (just as Israel communicated to the ancient Near East). To protect God's divinity, they said only God could *create*. Furthermore, with *creating* increasingly defined as *giving being*, creatures could not participate in creating, especially *ex nihilo*. In the biblical context, in which *Creator* meant having authority as Ruler over all things, the function of Creator was also limited to God alone. The difference is that the resulting situation that God purposes as Ruler does not have to be brought into being entirely by God alone. As Creator-Ruler,

God could call the land to put forth plants and animals; it is to function in support of those inhabitants. God alone had authority to declare that function. However, the resulting situation of having plants and animals supported by the land required obedience from God's subject (the land). It is true that God alone is Creator-Ruler and that creation only happens because of God's direct involvement, but it is not true that God alone accomplishes every result. God's *creation* of each thing is for it to function lovingly within the community so that all creation shines out of God's indwelling glory. God's creative rule includes all things actively and obediently loving God and neighbor. The end (creaturely participation) includes the means (creaturely participation).

When the Bible opens, there is nothing that will be God's heavens and earth (even the darkness is not yet night, and the waters are not yet seas); yet the Spirit of God is already present. The Spirit of God, from the Father, anticipates and also acts as impetus for creation. "The Spirit is willing" to enter the depths (Mark 14:38), "the wind blows where it will" (John 3:8), and the Spirit is present in creation's brokenness, groaning in intercession toward redemption (Rom. 8:22–27). This is the Spirit by which we come to participate in God's kingdom (John 3:5), to understand the things of the kingdom (1 Cor. 2:9–14), and to participate in resurrection life (new creation; Rom. 8:11). Only by the Spirit can we cry out *"Abba,* Father" (Rom. 8:15; Gal. 4:6; see Mark 14:36). The Spirit comes in advance as the possibility of creation's responsive participation. By the Spirit, God opens the possibility of something else's expression, beyond God's own.[7] God, by the Spirit, breathes

---

7. Many of the ideas in this section I explain in more detail in "Creation out of Nothing Remodeled," *Theologies of Creation*, 53–67, esp. 60–65. See also Vail, *Creation and Chaos Talk*, esp. chapter 6, "A New *Creatio ex Nihilo* Framework."

in all things toward participation in divine and creaturely communion; God also breathes them out beyond themselves in loving action for God and neighbor.[8]

The Father speaks the Word into the empty wilderness (the no-world) where the Spirit is already stirring. In the Gospels, as the incarnate Word was baptized and anointed by the Spirit, he went on the winds of the Spirit into the wilderness (Mark 1:12); later he went to the cross (Mark 14:36). Just as Christ pronounced that the kingdom of God was at hand, the Word pronounced from the beginning God's creative will. Making known divine purposes and wisdom for the world anticipates and invites obedient response. Certainly, God is at work in the unfolding community.[9] Yet, for the world itself, the Word acts less as a script than as *torah*—that is, God's statute and instruction, the wise path by which to walk. The Word goes ahead as the Way through whom we participate in and savor divine fellowship. We do not exist by being one-sidedly acted upon or by a command external to us; rather, in the potent presence of the Spirit and Word, creation has agency to express its own word. God and God's creation are all meant to act toward the fulfillment of God's good purposes. Creation unfolds in response to God.

The Spirit of God is the possibility for responsive participation; the Word of God is the call to which creation responds. We respond by the Spirit to the will of God mediated in and though the Word. Creation's response is only possible by God's Spirit, and creation is meant to unfold in relation to God's call. God inhabits creation as the possibility that it can express itself in love, wisdom, righteousness, and beauty. This seems to be the case as much

---

8. Brent D. Peterson, *Created to Worship* (Kansas City, MO: Beacon Hill Press of Kansas City, 2012).

9. God especially takes care of every feature of the heavens.

in the beginning—as the possibility for a beginning—as in creation's unfolding journey with our indwelling Redeemer-Creator-Ruler. God's Being does not have to project into existence the space, time, and material of the heavens and earth, nor does God have to declare it to exist in the exact specifications of God's sovereign blueprints. God is not pushing forth creation, dictating it, or giving creation a set of prewritten options from which to choose. Rather, from before God's creation—ahead of it and in front of it—God calls out for creation to act.[10]

Creation does not capture the Spirit or harness the Spirit. The Word does not become incarnated as creaturely existence. God and creation have distinct existence and agency. Even so, through God's own self-giving, the Spirit and Word make possible our own agency and word—a response that can be loving and good. The Spirit blows through or across, and the Word operates *trans*-carnately.[11] We are engaged by God, while also not being the stopping point of God's creative, sustaining activity. God makes our life possible, moving *through* and *in* every component of creation.[12] The very nature of the heavens and the earth (its origin, life, and end) is that all things would express them-

---

10. "God makes possible that an other might speak *with* God into the void. . . . God awaits the activity of the other that God makes possible; God awaits the word [the response] that creation expresses in coming-to-be. This word that is conceived as it is expressed by God's other is something new for God to know that is not of God's own concocting but made possible by God" (Vail, "Creation out of Nothing Remodeled," 61).

11. Vail, "Creation out of Nothing Remodeled," 62.

12. English prepositions are limited in helping us imagine God's activity. Perhaps we should say God works *"throughin"* creation. "*Through* by itself can carry too much the notion of a passing intersection with little or no interaction, unless it is taken in the sense of 'by means of.' *Throughout* can carry too much the notion of extension versus dynamic relation. Using *in* can be confusing in that either creation would be a container for God or there could be misunderstanding that the Word *in*carnates as the substance and/or form of creation or the Spirit is creation's subjectivity and/or expressed by creation" (Vail, *Creation and Chaos Talk*, 191–92; –see also Vail, *Eschatology*, 53–54).

selves in relation to God's own self-expression in Spirit and Word. Out of and in relation to God's outpoured love, we are most fundamentally oriented beyond ourselves to operate in love toward God and neighbor. "God gifts God's-self trans-creation that all creation might express itself in love toward God and neighbor."[13] God's intention for our very existence is for us to care for others, to live oriented beyond ourselves. As we arise from within the web of communal relations, we exist for that same community.

It is possible to keep continuity in God's renewing-creating-governing activities all the way through, even at the dawn of creation *ex nihilo*. Even at the beginning, God's loving activity makes possible "a *word from the other* in the creative event, an other who *does not preexist* the very creative activity of God itself."[14] God keeps acting so that something can exist (or unfold) that did not exist before, or would not exist otherwise. All the way through, God's active presence is redeeming-creating-governing for creation's flourishing. Even so, God's governance as Creator-Redeemer does not mean God alone brings about the result. God is making a creation where the whole community, comprising God and all parts of creation, is functioning lovingly to foster flourishing.

God is always giving God's very self in Spirit and Word toward all creation being bountifully alive in the full glory of God's triune love. However, since the situations that result from God's creative governance include responses from all parts of creation, things can unfold poorly. This is not God's doing. God continually provides, according to God's loving kindness, what creation needs. However, every single part of creation is not always fully expressive of God's loving purposes. Sometimes actors and whole systems express

---

13. Vail, "Creation out of Nothing Remodeled," 63.
14. Vail, *Creation and Chaos Talk*, 197.

themselves contrary to God's loving self-gift and intention. For example, DNA mutates in harmful ways, bacteria can shift from being helpful contributors in an ecosystem to agents of disease, and humankind multiplies ways to be self-serving agents of destruction. God's creatures can stand against their Redeemer-Creator-Ruler and blaspheme the only possibility for life and flourishing they have. By working against their God-given function, they are undone, and they are undoing their neighbors and the community as a whole.[15] The one suffering may not be the sinner. Even saints suffer because other parts of God's creation go astray.

Much of Christianity has emphasized God being the direct, creative cause of all things. This emphasis certainly helps us understand that we are a good creation and that our Creator is involved with every part of creation. There is a love relationship between Creator and creature. Love of neighbor has sometimes seemed like an add-on command. We might think, *Since we exist in this divine-creature relationship, perhaps we should look around and extend love to things around us.* However, if all things are called from within and for a community of love with God and neighbor, our every response across every moment is equally in relation to God and neighbor. What we are as agents, as well as the character of the whole community, is a complex unfolding of relations with God and neighbor. Whether we respond in the love of God or in disobedience, it shapes the whole community of creation. Our existence is supported and

---

15. For Christianity, "evil possesses no proper substance or nature of its own." Evil is certainly a reality in the world, but it is believed to be "a corruption and perversion of something that in its own proper nature is essentially good." God is not the source. "Evil is the creature of our choices, not of God's creative will. . . . All suffering, sadness, and death, however deeply woven into the fabric of earthly existence, is the consequence of the depravities of rational creatures, not of God's intentions" (David Bentley Hart, "The Devil's March: *Creatio ex nihilo*, the Problem of Evil, and a Few Dostoyevskian Meditations," *Creation* ex nihilo, 298, 299).

shaped by webs of creaturely expression in relation to God and neighbor; in turn, we constantly shape the nature of the community in our actions toward God and neighbor.[16] God is not our lone constituting relationship. The whole of creation is characterized by the ebb and flow of actions all community members make toward God and neighbor.

God invites forth a free creation that is neither tame nor scripted. That is the nature of the creation that God is making possible to unfold in relation to and enjoyment of God's own triune love. God also has agency to act in the community. God is Creator of this self-expressive creation, and God is a fellow actor in the story. God makes Godself known and also works in the community. God can build up, tear down, water, and prune as our Ruler-Redeemer who is working for the world's thriving.[17] God has God's own life and makes our life possible. We are dependent on God's continual, immediate activity, even while God maintains God's integrity as a distinct agent from us.[18] Our alienation from God and neighbor, our suffering, and our warfare will all come to an end when God's glory fully inhabits creation, creation is entirely renewed, and we all walk by the Spirit in the light of God and the Lamb.

Talking with Science

As mentioned in the previous chapter, there are many ways that our present scientific context should excite Christians. It has been a long time since the broader scientific

---

16. Relationship with God and neighbor are not operating on different planes or running in different directions (like vertical and horizontal). They are all part of the same dynamic of fellowship in God's temple sanctuary. See Severson, *Scandalous Obligation*, 160–73.

17. For descriptions of God's actions to discipline and cultivate creation toward fulfillment, see Vail, *Eschatology*, 55–78.

18. The incarnation is all the more profound in that God crosses into creaturely existence to act as creation instead of *through in* it, or as an agent entirely distinct from it.

accounts were a good fit for conversation with the biblical imagination about God and creation. Science has moved away from seeing processes of physics as mechanical and lifeless. Things interact with each other in ways that are not linear and deterministic. The ways in which processes unfold are akin to all things in creation being God's subjects. While not everything is a conscious, thinking subject, God may indeed be making possible that all features of God's creation are responsive to God's in-breathing, calling activity—including subatomic particles and inorganic materials.[19] Whether the sciences are speaking about the unfolding of the universe over billions of years or the unfolding of life on Earth, the biblical imagination about creation's unfolding is valid. God's activity is necessary for any of it to be possible, God has purposes for creation's function, and every component has an active role to play. Biblical theology can comfortably dialogue with theories of the big bang, quantum mechanics, and evolutionary biology.

The movement in the sciences toward studying systems rather than lone subjects is also a better fit for biblical conversation than earlier periods in Western history. God's provision is for a world that is interdependent, where all things function within and for the flourishing of the whole community; every piece has a function in relation to something else. Science is moving toward this vision and can help Christians understand the marvelous complexities and interconnectedness of God's creation.

It has only been in the last hundred years that scientists and mathematicians were able to demonstrate that the

---

19. On the contribution of earth's minerals to the unfolding of life on the planet, see Maya Wei-Haas, "Life and Rocks May Have Co-Evolved on Earth," *Smithsonian Magazine* (January 13, 2016), https://www.smithsonianmag.com/science-nature/life-and-rocks-may-have-co-evolved-on-earth-180957807/; and *Life's Rocky Start: PBS Nova Documentary Collection*, https://youtu.be/zA4w0b2WRvo.

universe had a beginning.[20] Through all the centuries of Christianity, theologians merely had to take the Bible at its word that there was a beginning. A good number of theologians and philosophers speculated that there was no logical reason the universe could not have always existed. The work of mathematicians and astrophysicists in the twentieth century finally provided evidence for a beginning point.

Rather than seeing science as the enemy, there are so many ways that present theories within science make a great pairing with biblical imagination. If anything, the knowledge that science provides only helps us better act for the good of the world and its inhabitants, in fulfillment of the purpose for which God created humankind.

God's Economy

We have too long put the doctrine of creation at the beginning of the world's timeline, a long distance from where we stand. The biblical doctrine of creation, however, is interested in creation as the basis for our ultimate redemption hopes and our present life in the world. We are to live now in light of who we are meant to be as subjects of this particular Redeemer-Creator-Ruler. There are at least a few practices in Western culture that the biblical doctrine of creation questions.

First, nothing in creation exists for self-benefit or to be an end user—including humankind. Humankind was created to image God, which means we were created to give of ourselves for the flourishing of the earth and its inhabitants. We were not created to become consumers of the earth and its inhabitants—only ministers to them. The

---

20. Stephen M. Barr, "Modern Cosmology and Christian Theology," *Blackwell Companion to Science and Christianity*, ed. J. B. Stump and Alan G. Padgett (Chinchester, UK: John Wiley & Sons, 2012), 178–79. Thank you, Luke Couchman, for this reference.

only thing we were given to consume is the vegetation that is graciously provided. God's economy is an economy of giving and receiving. We receive, and we give.

Second, humankind is never given ownership of the land and the animals. The kingdom is always God's. We govern on behalf of God, in the likeness of God. When Israel inhabited the promised land, it was never *their* property. Each family had a portion that provided for the family's needs as they tended it for its own health. *Sales* of the land really only functioned as long-term leases of the land until oversight returned to the family at the Year of Jubilee. Israel could not do with the land, the animals, or anyone in the land as they saw fit. All things belong to God, are God's subjects, and are for the purposes God has given them. We are to operate through all times of the day—in every day, season, and year—according to God's life-thriving *torah*. The earth, the things that grow, and every inhabitant are not "natural resources" for us to determine what they are for or how to use them. We are not to bend them to our own purposes for self-gain. We ourselves are of the land, inhabitants of the land, and for the land. We are meant to learn from God what things are for and do for God's creation what best helps it thrive.

Third, Christians should be the most attentive protectors of animals and the natural environment. With any species or habitat, we should be the fastest to respond to distress or threats we detect. "The whole creation has been groaning" and "waits in eager expectation for the children of God to be revealed" (Rom. 8:22, 19). The best advocates for and practitioners of environmental protection, environmental justice, and sustainable living should be Christians. In our jobs and communities, Christians should be on the leading edge of practices that benefit the soil, air, water, and animals. Christians should have dominion as our Ruler-Redeemer does and be healers of the seas, the land, animal-kind, and humankind. In God's kingdom, sicknesses and oppression in bodies and relationships are rectified (Matt. 4:23; Luke 9:2; 10:8–9); Christians are meant to be ambassadors of God's reconciling reign (2 Cor. 5:17–20). While full redemption will take place at Christ's return, the body of Christ is meant to participate in and bear faithful witness in our conduct to the truth of God and God's unending kingdom.

Lastly, our whole life in the world should not only be lived in wisdom but should also be experienced sacramentally.[21] We receive many delights from God's many subjects. The gift is not just their loving and beautiful response, but it is also enabled out of God's in-filling love. Acknowledging God's indwelling moves us from the immediate experience into thanks and praise to God. Our vision includes the God of all grace. Every experience within creation is opportunity for fellowship with fellow creation and Creator. All creation is God's sanctuary. We should not cut God out of our vision of life or operate as if time, space, or work were created to be secular. All blessings are from God, in union with fellow creation, to the glorification of God.

No god that any humans have ever imagined is anything as wonderful as the true, living God. Those gods ask for service without returning true well-being and flourishing for all. Those gods dominate, leaving the earth and the multitudes to function only for the benefit of the gods and the elect. There is truly no god like our God. "The LORD is good to all; he has compassion on all he has made" (Ps. 145:9). Our Redeemer-Creator-Ruler is love. God is self-giving and other-nurturing. God acts in the Word made flesh, by the Holy Spirit, for us and our salvation. Our God en-

---

21. Lodahl and Maskiewicz, *Renewal in Love*, 69–110; Alexander Schmemann, *For the Life of the Word* (Crestwood, NY: St. Vladimir's Seminary Press, 1973).

dures all things—even death—for all creation to participate in the resurrection blessing of God's glorious love, without end. Join the chorus of "every creature in heaven and on earth and under the earth and on the sea, and all that is in them, saying: 'To him who sits on the throne and to the Lamb be praise and honor and glory and power, for ever and ever!'" (Rev. 5:13). Amen!

www.ingramcontent.com/pod-product-compliance
Lightning Source LLC
Chambersburg PA
CBHW061941220426
43662CB00012B/1982